**SIX ESSAYS
ON VAUXHALL
GARDENS**

SIX ESSAYS ON VAUXHALL GARDENS

DAVID E. COKE

SERIES EDITOR
Naomi Clifford

Copyright © 2022 David E. Coke
ISBN 978 1 9196232 2 1

The right of David E. Coke to be identified as the author of this work has been asserted by him in accordance with the Copyright, Designs and Patents Act, 1988.

A CIP record for this book is available from the British Library.

All rights reserved. No part of this book may be reproduced or transmitted in any form or by any means, electronic or mechanical including photocopying, recording, or by any information storage and retrieval system, without permission from the Publisher in writing.

Published in association with The Vauxhall Society
vauxhallcivicsociety.org.uk   vauxhallhistory.org

Caret Press
9 Durand Gardens, London SW9 0PS
info@caretpress.com   caretpress.com

DAVID E. COKE F.S.A. is a consulting editor at and contributor to VauxhallHistory.org, the history offshoot of The Vauxhall Society.

Between 1976 and 1979 he was curator of Gainsborough's House in Sudbury, Suffolk, where he organised the exhibition The Muses' Bower: Vauxhall Gardens 1728–1786. While Director of Pallant House Gallery, Chichester (1981–1997) he curated the Vauxhall Gardens section in the 1984 Rococo exhibition at the Victoria & Albert Museum, London and in 2012 The Triumph of Pleasure, an exhibition for the Foundling Museum, London.

David's many publications include *Vauxhall Gardens: A History* (with Dr Alan Borg Yale, University Press, 2011); 'Patriotism and Pleasure', for *History Today*, May 2012; 'Roubiliac's Handel for Vauxhall Gardens: A sculpture in context', *The Sculpture Journal*; a section on twentieth-century art in *Chichester Cathedral—An Historical Survey*, ed. Mary Hobbs (Phillimore, 1994); a section on pleasure gardens for the Oxford Companion to Gardens (1986); the Vauxhall Gardens section in Rococo–Art and Design in *Hogarth's England 1728–1786* (V&A, 1984); *The Muses' Bower, Vauxhall Gardens 1728–1786*, the catalogue for the exhibition at Gainsborough's House.

SIX ESSAYS

	Introduction	*viii*
1	The surprising career of C.H. Simpson, Master of Ceremonies 1797–1835	*2*
2	Vauxhall Gardens in contemporary children's board games	*30*
3	Evanion–the 'Royal Conjuror', supplier of refreshments to Vauxhall and obsessive collector of entertainment ephemera	*44*
4	New evidence of the popular nostalgia for Vauxhall after it closed	*62*
5	The record-breaking flight of the Royal Vauxhall Balloon in 1836	*72*
6	Tracking the fate of Vauxhall's outdoor bandstand	*94*

INTRODUCTION

THIS BOOK IS a compilation of some of the essays written following the publication of David E. Coke and Alan Borg's *Vauxhall Gardens: A History*. One of the most problematic and painful aspects of preparing that book, Coke tells us, was the necessity to edit it down to a manageable size, which of course meant losing many of the most fascinating topics and stories. So this sequel was conceived partly to expand subjects only mentioned in the book, and partly to explore those subjects that the book had to lose altogether, or even subjects the author was unaware of at the time of publication. Although the six essays included here stand on their own quite happily, they were really intended as pendants to the 2011 book, or to the 'Brief History' published on Coke's website at vauxhallgardens.com.

Other 'extramural' essays on Vauxhall by Coke have been published in periodicals–notably 'Roubiliac's Handel for Vauxhall Gardens: a sculpture in context' in *The Sculpture Journal*,[1] and '"Vauxhall Gardens in an Uproar": the Reinhold Affair of 1750' in *The London Journal*.[2] As with the six essays in this book, the two earlier articles were based on new research, combined, where appropriate, with earlier scholarship, and extensively illustrated. The 'Reinhold Affair' concerned a very unusual public row between the proprietor and the musicians which caused a musicians' strike, leaving Vauxhall without music for the only time in its history.

As well as a cultural historian, Coke is an obsessive collector of all things to do with the two great commercial pleasure gardens of Georgian London–Vauxhall in Lambeth and Ranelagh Gardens in Chelsea; in the process of collecting, new discoveries are occasionally made, and he believes that these should be shared with scholars as soon and as accessibly as possible. Both the essay on board games, and the one on Henry Evans Evanion were prompted by such new and exciting discoveries.

Through his website, and through his close association with the Foundling Museum in Bloomsbury, Coke receives regular enquiries from individuals and institutions interested in particular aspects of the pleasure gardens, and this, too, has prompted new writing–'The Career of C.H. Simpson', as well as other articles on the Vauxhall History website have arisen from intriguing enquiries from members of the public.

Other shorter articles are inspired by unanswered questions prompted by Coke's own collecting. What is the provenance of an intriguing watercolour of the coach entrance at Vauxhall Gardens? And what happened to the Vauxhall Orchestra building after it was sold for £90 at the final dispersal auction in 1859? Some of these questions will never be answered, but unless they are asked, we will never know.

Vauxhall Gardens was a significant element in the social lives of Londoners for the best part of two centuries, from the 1660s until 1859. Jonathan Tyers, its greatest proprietor (between 1729 and 1759), was not only a brilliant businessman but also one of the most important patrons of the arts in Georgian Britain. Without Tyers and his successors, British music, art and entertainments would be significantly poorer. As a result, the serious study of Vauxhall and the other London pleasure gardens is at last becoming a reputable pursuit. We hope that *Six Essays* will add to the growing body of knowledge around Vauxhall, and may even prompt further research and writing on the subject.

NAOMI CLIFFORD, *Series Editor*
ROSS DAVIES, *The Vauxhall Society*

THE SURPRISING CAREER OF
C.H. SIMPSON
MASTER *of* CEREMONIES
1797–1835

The patrons of the Royal Gardens, Vauxhall, will regret to learn that a Gentleman (Mr Simpson) whose name and person have for so many years been associated with that popular scene of recreation, is no more. The well-known 'Master of Ceremonies,' who has filled that distinguished post for 38 years, to the infinite advantage of the Proprietors, and gratification of the public, departed this life on Friday, the 25th ult.

The Examiner, Sunday 3 January 1836

THIS IS ONE of many published notices of the death of one of Vauxhall's great historic characters. C.H. Simpson, as he was universally known, was born Christopher Herbert Simpson, the fourth son of George and Dorothy; he was baptised, like his three elder brothers and younger sister, in the parish of St George, Bloomsbury. A shorter obituary appeared in the prestigious *Gentleman's Magazine*'s Deaths column: '25 December 1835. Mr. C.H. Simpson, late Master of the Ceremonies of the Royal Gardens, Vauxhall; so long the butt of the newspaper wits, and well-known from his grotesque whole-length portrait. He had served in the Royal Navy.'[3]

As Master of Ceremonies at Vauxhall, Simpson was widely known and recognised by the character he assumed. Exquisitely dressed in old-fashioned costume, his obsequious civility to everybody, whoever they

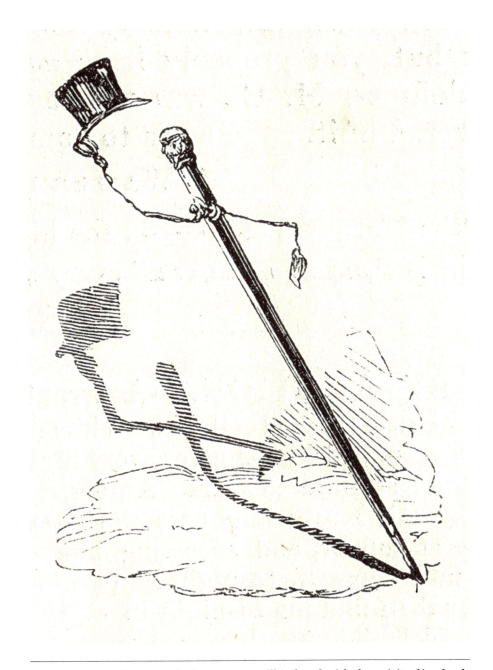

FIG.1 Cartoon of Simpson's ebony cane, still imbued with the spirit of its dead owner, and raising its hat with a tasselled 'arm' to an imaginary visitor. *From Alfred Bunn and Alfred Crowquill's Vauxhall Papers (1841), No.2, p.15.* CVRC 0182.

were, and whatever they had done, became proverbial. His deep bow of welcome 'to the Royal Property' (i.e. Vauxhall Gardens), exercised after a polite step back to allow space for the elegant sweep of his arm, was indiscriminately received by anybody standing close enough. We are assured that Simpson was 'endowed with ubiquity', as he appeared to be everywhere in the Gardens at once. 'He has attended here... every public night from eight at night until three in the morning for above twenty years!' Whenever there was any sort of disturbance, 'He pierces through the mob like an eel in mud' to calm things down.[4]

Simpson's panache and civility did have a practical application; a news report of 1833, reports a disturbance at Vauxhall, caused by

> a party of 'peep-a-day boys' (hooligans) who had been drinking heavily. One of them was a big, powerful youth, who discouraged any attempts by waiters or others to get in his way. The call went out for Simpson, who came out and made a most profound bow to the riotous swain, who, on seeing Simpson's hat flourishing in the air, his fine oval powdered cranium bare, cried out, with a thundering voice 'who the h—l are you?'–the M.C. bowing to the ground, answered with the greatest complacency 'Your very obedient humble servant'–'You be d—d.'; Simpson: 'Sir, you do me honour.' Buck: 'Honour, the d—l.' Simpson: 'Sir, you are perfectly right, he ought to be honour'd.' Buck: 'Who ought to be honour'd and be d—d to you.' Simpson: 'Your own noble and generous self, who are the most good naturest gentleman I know.' Buck: 'What do you know of me, you puppy.' Simpson: 'Every thing that is valiant, courageous and manly.' Another profound bow, hat off, which the ungracious youth kicked into the air; but the peace-making philosopher, quickly picked it up–replaced it on his head, with that elegance of gait and manner so peculiar to himself, that it made even the rebel to smile, of which the M.C. taking advantage, addressed him thus, 'Sir, you are little aware that I have the honour to know your noble relatives; his lordship, your extinguished father, is a great patron of the Royal Property; on that account, permit me, right honourable sir, to conduct you to your carriage: clear the way there, lamplighters and waiters, don't commode his honour; this way, highly respected sir, this way.'– The youth tickled with the high rank the witty M.C. had bestowed on him, suffered himself to be led out of the Gardens like a lamb.[5]

This was not the behaviour of an innocent or an idiot, but of a highly-practised diplomat and serviceman, well used to keeping order without aggression or violence – an ability of great skill.

By his own account, and confirmed by the historical record, Simpson had indeed served in the Navy as a boy. Between 1781/2 and 1783, he served as a young midshipman on board the new ship, the seventy-four-gun *Warrior,* under its commander Captain Sir James Wallace, a friend of his father's. In this situation he saw combat, under Admiral Rodney, on 12 April 1782 at the 'bloody and furious battle' of Saintes in the West Indies, when the French fleet was soundly defeated and their admiral, the Count de Grasse, was captured. On 12 July he is marked as discharged, but the ship's cash book shows he received his full wages of £61. 19s. 10d., paid on 21 July; he returned to England, after more naval service, in 1783.

Simpson's naval career is reported in his address to the public on the occasion of his great benefit night at Vauxhall in 1833 (the printed address was on sale at sixpence per copy), but what the young C.H. Simpson did for the years between 1783 and 1797 is one of the mysteries that surround him. Vauxhall had strong connections with the London theatres, sharing several performers in common, and there were, at the time, several actors in London called Simpson, one of them even with the same distinctive pair of initials; C.H. Simpson the actor performed at the Adelphi Theatre in London between 1809 and 1820, but there is also a mention in 1787 of a Mr Simpson playing a valet in a pantomime called *Hobson's Choice* at the Royalty Theatre in Well Street (just to the east of the Tower of London). This may have been the better-known actor George Simpson, who died in 1795, but it seems an unusually minor role for such a figure at that time. Another record of an actor called Simpson places him at the Theatre Royal Brighton before 1809, where he was playing dashing young men or soldiers. Who is to say today but that a young character actor may have seen in the comic portrayal of the valet the embryo of a much more important role, even down to the costume?

It is entirely conceivable, although impossible now to prove, that Christopher Simpson, a competent jobbing actor may have decided to give up the allure of many insecure roles on the late Georgian stage for the security of the starring role at Vauxhall Gardens. To suggest that 'C.H. Simpson, Master of Ceremonies at the Royal Gardens, Vauxhall' was a role that Simpson chose to act is by no means to denigrate his achievements. His was one of the great comic theatrical roles of the nineteenth century, known and loved by a huge number of people, and equal to anything invented by Vesta Tilley or Dan Leno in the music halls, by Kenneth Williams in the *Carry On* films, or indeed among the television soap stars of more recent times.

The success of Simpson's transformation was achieved by a double disguise–his determined hiding of his Christian name behind those initials, and his invariable uniform when seen in public–an undoubtedly theatrical and old-fashioned costume of black buckled knee-breeches and stockings, patent pumps with black bows, a white waistcoat and black morning coat, all close-fitting, with a cascading cravat at his neck, a watch-chain loaded with seals and fobs, an occasional seasonal nosegay at the button-hole, and a black beaver hat on (or most often courteously lifted off) his bald head; the ensemble was completed with white gloves and a tasselled silver-mounted ebony cane (*Fig.1*)–a character costume if ever there was one. The costume is first visually recorded in the portrait of Simpson created by J.W. Gear for his 1833 Benefit Night at Vauxhall (*Fig.2*), and is celebrated in poetry by a contemporary versifier:

On the Incomparable Portrait of the Inimitable
"C.H.Simpson, Esq., Master of Ceremonies at Vauxhall."
By the author of "Crayons From the Commons."

The painter's art unrivall'd we behold,
In seizing all that Nature's hand could mould –
In tracing forth each point on which we gaze,
While matchless Simpson fills us with amaze –
Simpson, who stands proclaim'd, by one and all,
The glorious guardian genius of Vauxhall!
That saltant form, with agile gait, appears,
A prancing comment on advancing years;
That face, despite of wrinkles, rude is seen,
A strong, perennial, stubborn evergreen.
The more we gaze, the more must we admire
Each nicer touch that pencils his attire:
His pliant pumps upon their surface show
Two tasteful knots, full bunching to a bow;
His silken hose are soften'd on the sight,
In sable contrast with the buckle bright,

Which, in its sparkling vividness, we see
Reflecting transient lustre from his knee;
His coat enhances his transcendant vest –
A costly brilliant blazes on his breast;
His hat, with rim convolv'd on either side,
Completes the acmé of his conscious pride.
But all the powers of graphic song were vain
To tune each movement of his ebon cane,
As onward still in greeting mood he trips,
The "Royal Gardens" on his lauding lips.
Ne'er could the Muse, in numbers meet, pourtray
The prostrate homage, studious of display,
Evinc'd, as each beholder must allow,
Within the circle of his sweeping bow.
These features rare the Sister Art alone
Describes, by means peculiarly her own:
Fam'd Simpson swells in ev'ry cut and caper,
The crowning climax of pictorial paper.
Such the great man whom fashion proudly stamps,
Flaming beneath five hundred thousand lamps.

JUST AS THE real Jonathan Tyers, the temperamental and depressive founder of the Gardens in the 1730s, had to hide behind the mask of the urbane host and gentleman patron of the arts, so the real C.H. Simpson, doubtless scarred by his brief but violent experience of warfare as a child of twelve, and depressed by his lack of acting success, hid himself behind the comic figure of his Master of Ceremonies–what Thackeray in *Vanity Fair* called 'The gentle Simpson, that kind smiling idiot'. This character became famous for his excessive and unfailing politeness to everybody, an obsessive courtesy and ridiculous, fawning sycophancy; invariable behaviour that visitors would travel for miles just to see and to experience. Simpson was a phenomenon, a wonder, a spectacle in his own right; such was the impression made by his character that he soon morphed into a trade-mark for Vauxhall, a universally recognised logo. This fact was exploited and encouraged by John William Gear (c.1799–1866) painter, printer, and publisher, who created the full-length lithograph portrait of Simpson (*see Fig.2*), first issued in 1831 for sale at the gardens, and referred to by *The Gentleman's Magazine* as 'grotesque', which here means something more akin to 'caricature'. As Simpson himself had an interest in its sale, he wrote letters, in his own idiosyncratic style, to his friends in the press: 'Highly esteemed Sir—With a heart filled with every sentiment of the most profound gratitude for all your manifold kindnesses to me, I most respectfully, and in the most humble and submissive manner, entreat, kind Sir, that your well-known goodness of heart will be graciously pleased to condescend to accept the enclosed portrait of myself.'

He goes on to explain that the print is for sale at two shillings, and to ask the editor to write up the print in his next edition.[6] This, of course, following such a polite entreaty, they were delighted to do. Simpson's marketing skills were not far short of those of Jonathan Tyers himself, and used to equal effect—further evidence of the intelligence and skills of the man behind the disguise.

The genius of Gear's composition is that it is not a straight portrait, but rather a full-length silhouette, catching the sitter from his left side in his characteristic pose, about to bow to a visitor, his right foot behind the left, his hat lifted, his cane held off the floor like a staff of office, creating one of the most striking and memorable portraits of the period.

So memorable was the silhouette that it went on to inspire another, possibly even more famous logo; when the cartoonist Tom Browne was commissioned to produce a marketing device for a Scotch whisky company in 1908, he brought Gear's portrait to mind and created the famous 'Striding Man' logo for Johnnie Walker. Reinforcing this link, a magazine advertisement for the Scotch in the 1930s actually adapted the 1833 Robert Cruikshank scene of Simpson welcoming the Duke of Wellington to Vauxhall against the backdrop of the Orchestra and the gigantic illuminated figure of Simpson created for his benefit night (*Fig.3*), replacing the illuminated Simpson with the new figure. With its strapline of 'Born 1820... still going strong', Johnnie Walker's early publicity regularly harked back to an earlier more elegant age, and Vauxhall Gardens, itself still going strong in 1820 and after, fitted the bill very well (*Fig.4*).

The Gear silhouette was adapted by other artists, especially in designs for Vauxhall's publicity. The best example of this is the handbill advertising the Grand Coronation Gala of 9 September 1833, the

FIG.2 W. Day after John William Gear, C.H. Simpson Esqre. Thirty Four Years Master of the Ceremonies at the Royal Gardens Vauxhall; "Welcome to the Royal Property". *(1831) Lithograph.* CVRC 0579.

closing night of the season, headed by Simpson's striding figure (*Fig.5*). Everybody would have been immediately aware that this was a Vauxhall handbill, but it also gave the image itself an added currency. The text of the handbill is in the form of a letter from Simpson to Vauxhall's patrons, in his usual obsequious style, designed, as always, to make people smile:

> To all those truly illustrious, noble, and distinguished Visitors of the Royal Gardens, Vauxhall, their truly humble and very devoted Servant, C.H. Simpson, Master of the Ceremonies at those Gardens for Thirty-six Years, most dutifully and most respectfully begs to inform all the illustrious, noble, and all the other respectable classes that visit the Royal Gardens, that I am directed by the worthy Proprietors to announce the closing of the Royal Gardens on Monday next... (*Fig.6*)

The 'letter' goes on to enumerate the attractions of the Coronation Gala in a similar style.

Even such a distinguished artist as George Cruikshank borrowed the image, realising that it was a useful shorthand for the location; in his *Comic Almanack* for July 1835, the main illustration shows a crowded Vauxhall Gardens, as viewed from the entrance to the Rotunda looking south, with the recognisable figure in the centre, bowing to a middle-class couple, much to the amazement of a rustic couple behind him, obviously on their first visit (*Fig.7*).

> Simpson, of bowing and letter-writing celebrity, was for years an attraction. It is impossible to conceive anything more solemnly absurd, more inexpressibly ludicrous, than this little fellow, who paraded in the gardens in unexceptionable black tights, carrying his beaver up a foot above his head, and bowing to everything he saw, animate or inanimate, from a lord to a lamp-post...
>
> *The Sunday Times*, 6 October 1844

This is the kind of publicity that Simpson's character consistently gained for Vauxhall throughout his career, and which made an incalculable contribution to the continuing success of the Gardens right up to the accession of Queen Victoria. Because of Simpson's starring role

FIG.3 Drawn in the Gardens, on the night of August the 19th. 1833, by Robert Cruikshank Esqr.' C.H. Simpson, EsqR. M.C.R.G.V. For upwards of 36 Years,–with a distant view of his Colossal Likeness in Variegated Lamps. To C.H. Simpson Esqr. M.C. of the Royal Gardens Vauxhall, this Print / taken in the Sixty Third year of his age, on the Night of his benefit is, by express permission,/ most respectfully dedicated by his obliged and humble Servant, the Publisher. / Price 1s.6d. Plain. 2s.6d. Col'd. *Etching and aquatint, hand coloured. Published by W. Kidd, 14 Chandos Street West, 20 August 1833.* CVRC 0669.

FIG.4 Full-page advertisement from an American periodical for Johnnie Walker Scotch Whisky *(1936)*. CVRC 0080.

at Vauxhall, and his ability to keep order, alongside major attractions like Charles Green's balloon ascents (*see pp.72–93*), Vauxhall Gardens could contribute hugely to the local economy of Vauxhall for several decades beyond its realistic expectations.

FIRST EMPLOYED AT Vauxhall Gardens aged only twenty-seven, Simpson stayed in post for the remarkable total of thirty-eight years, a reign as long and as notable as that of Jonathan Tyers himself. Even though he was employed from the opening night of 1797 (3 June), it is not until much later that we hear anything significant about him. This appears to be because his earlier role at the Gardens was not as much in the public eye as it later became. When he appeared at the Surrey Magistrates Quarter Sessions on 14 October 1811 as the 'accuser', along with constable James Glannon, of three of Vauxhall's lamplighters for stealing lamp-oil and wick-cotton, he was called the 'Superintendent at Vauxhall Gardens'; this makes absolute sense when taken together with the verse in 'Simpson the Beau' quoted below, where he is called the 'Chief inspector of fowls, ham and beef' and the taster of punch; he was, it appears, in charge of quality control of the refreshments, and maybe of the junior staff as well.

His first job at Vauxhall, then, was not Master of Ceremonies at all, but something more like a front-of-house manager, in which role, the public would have known little of him. Of the accused lamplighters, one was acquitted, one was found guilty and given three months hard labour, and the ring-leader of the gang, one Samuel Brown, was found guilty and sentenced to twelve months hard labour and public whipping for 150 yards in Kennington Lane.

As the front-of-house manager, Simpson would have worked alongside a business manager–soon after Simpson's arrival, the name of James Perkins (or Parkins) appears as 'manager' on insurance documents and other official and financial papers. During Simpson's time, the situation of business manager or treasurer changed hands many times. He also saw the proprietorship change hands from the great-grandsons of Jonathan Tyers to the business partnership of Frederick Gye and Richard Hughes.

Over the next decade or so, Simpson must have transformed his chosen job into something much more public, almost a *maître d'hôte,* in which the satisfaction of Vauxhall's customers, rather than the supervision of his juniors, became his main concern. From this, it would have been a short step to M.C., which is exactly what he is called in the in-house accounts for 1822/23, preserved in the Shaw collection at Harvard[7]; as M.C. he was earning £34 per season, with a bonus of £10. In addition, and in common with other members of the senior staff, Simpson was allowed free refreshments. The fact that he was employed for the season, rather than permanently, may suggest that he was still finding work, maybe on the stage, outside the Vauxhall season. His colleagues in 1823–the treasurer William Rouse and the manager Mr Ghent–both appear to have been full-time appointments, the first earning a salary of £500, and the second £100 per annum. The 1823 season ran from 19 May to 12 September–seventeen weeks in all, so Simpson's *pro rata* salary was the equivalent of Mr Ghent's.

We find no mention of Simpson in the press coverage of Vauxhall until the last night celebrations of the 1826 season, attended by seven hundred visitors. A newspaper report on the following day bemoans the fact that the proprietors had probably made very little profit that season, but 'To Mr Simpson, and indeed to every gentleman of the establishment, the thanks of the visitors are due for the zeal, promptitude and regularity with which their various duties have been executed.'[8] It was Simpson who received the credit for the smooth running of the gardens.

Just four years later, Simpson had already become the almost mythical 'presiding deity' at Vauxhall for which he is best known today, his behaviour and character well-worn subjects for comedy and satire. It was in its issue of 7 August 1830, only three weeks after the funeral of George IV, that *The Mirror of Literature, Amusement and Instruction* published a comic article called 'The Bower–A Vauxhall View.' Anybody reading that title would ordinarily have expected the subject to be the venerable pleasure garden itself, but the joke, possibly in its first of many appearances, was broken to the reader at the end of the first paragraph:

> The Bower that we allude to, is not that wherein hearts and promises are sometimes broken, which birds delight to haunt, and bards to describe. No, it is merely a human being, a living bower–an acquaintance most probably of the reader's;–we mean, in short, the Master of the Ceremonies at Vauxhall Gardens!

FIG. 5 Grand Coronation Gala handbill and detail (1833). CVRC 0676.

FIG. 6 Detail of Fig. 5. *An ink drawing in the Museum of London [Z2065], closely related to this version of the Simpson portrait, is signed 'C. Bridges'.*

FIG.7 George Cruikshank, 'July'. *From 'The Comic Almanack' (1835), opp. p.17.* CVRC 0437.

The *Mirror* article, while acknowledging that there were few people who did not know of Simpson as a civilised and civilising influence at Vauxhall, goes on to enumerate several mysteries about 'our kind and accomplished friend'. The writer describes how Simpson would appear like magic at your supper-box and politely enquire whether there was anything he could do to improve the evening of the visitors dining there. He describes Simpson's constant bowing and smiling, and wonders how he could keep it up quite so constantly, even when wine is spilled on his pumps or over his immaculate white waistcoat, at which 'he smiles as if you had conferred a favour on him, and bows himself dry again'. Another mystery was where Simpson went when it was not supper-time—he was seldom seen when not ensuring that visitors were enjoying their suppers. But the greatest mystery of all, according to *The Mirror*, was where Simpson disappeared to out of season—'He and the lights go out together'. The mystery was as great as that of the migrations of birds. It is now clear to historians that Simpson, during the Vauxhall season, rented rooms at 12 Lambeth Walk, and for the rest of the year returned to his own residence off the Mile End Road, more or less on the site of the present Harford Street. The address then was 4 Regent Place, from where Simpson wrote to his employer Frederick Gye in 1826 thanking him for his continued employment, and pointing out the 'truly enormous and almost useless expenditure' on Vauxhall's force of constables at that time.[9] Later he moved to more salubrious, though less rural, surroundings at 31 Holywell Street, Strand, where he is recorded by 1830.

While the letter to Frederick Gye is authenticated by the recipient, it is frequently difficult, because his writing style was so distinctive and so easily parodied, to determine whether published letters, articles or other writings signed by Simpson are, in fact, by him. There was a regular flow of writings in Simpson's idiosyncratic style, and, often, replies and disclaimers apparently from him as well, all lightly satirical. This makes it hard to ascertain what is true and what is not. The climax of this series is Simpson's 'autobiography', called *The Surprising Life and Adventures of C. H. Simpson, Master of the Ceremonies at the Royal Gardens, Vauxhall, from his earliest Youth to the sixty-Fifth Year of his Age. Written by Myself, and dedicated to my friend, the Editor of "The Times"*, published by W. Strange in 1835. This is a very kind parody, gently comic even today, and completely inoffensive. Its *leitmotif*, repeated many times, is the fact that he was Master of the Ceremonies at Vauxhall for thirty-eight years, and that he is now in the sixty-fifth year of his life. The autobiography (only thirty-odd pages in all) is repetitive, abject, self-effacing, effusive, self-caricaturing; the subject sometimes clearly mistakes criticism for praise, and teasing for friendship. It is entirely possible, even probable, that all these 'hoax' writings, even including the *Mirror* article, were actually by Simpson himself, as self-caricature. If I am right in assuming that his 'Master of Ceremonies' was a character role he created and adopted, then it is equally likely that the various writings signed by him, even the 'autobiography' were merely building up that character, making it better-known and better loved – all part of his continuing campaign to promote the Gardens. The C.H. Simpson 'so long the butt of the newspaper wits', as *The Gentleman's Magazine* put it, may quite credibly have been entirely the creation of a minor actor best known for comedy valets or dapper young gentlemen.

His date of birth is given in his autobiography as 1 April 1770, although we now know that this April Fools' Day birthday is part of the author's joke. At least the year is correct, but the real date was just a week earlier, 26 March. In early childhood, the author reports, Simpson had apparently so well mastered the art of bowing 'that my respected, elegant, and accomplished parents Denominated me "the Bower of Bliss"'. We are told that Simpson was considered 'a clever child' because he once burned his hands in the fire by accident 'and actually took them out again without being told, and this was considered very shrewd and clever in so young a Child'. One possibly mythical event of his childhood was carried in *The Magazine of Curiosity and Wonder* (an illustrated penny magazine produced by Thomas Prest and published by George Drake) in 1836, apparently quoting an earlier press report:

> Yesterday evening as the infant son of Mr. Simpson, residing in Westminster, was playing on a bed in the nursery, he was suddenly rolled off into a large tub, which was full of water, and in consequence of the size

FIG.8   George Balne, Handbill for Simpson's Benefit Night on 19 August 1833, with a small wood-engraved version of Gear's portrait. Below the image of Simpson is a long 'address to the public' from Simpson in his usual style, inviting their attendance; it includes some of his own life story, especially details about his naval service. CVRC 0641.

of the vessel, the accident would most certainly have been attended with fatal consequences, had not a fine dog, belonging to the family, observed the peril of the child, and rescued it from its dangerous situation.

Quoted from the *Morning Advertiser* of August 1773 in
The Magazine of Curiosity and Wonder, Thursday 7 January 1836[10]

The dog, named William Tell, lived on to great old age after this event. Even though this story stretches our credibility, there is enough factually correct material in the autobiography to suggest that the author, whether Simpson himself or not, knew a great deal about his subject.

'An interesting and unique Gala' at Vauxhall Gardens on 19 August 1833 marked the apogee of Simpson's long career (*Fig.8*). The attractions for the occasion included a huge illuminated transparent painting of the city of Antwerp, a 'water scene' representing the Triumph of Britannia 'amidst the Discharge of large bodies of Water, Explosion of Bombs, Shells, Rockets, Coloured Fires, &c., with music from the military band of the Grand Duke of Darmstadt'. It is for this spectacular occasion that the creation of Simpson's character was truly completed, and his myth made immortal. The first 'Benefit night' so far given to an individual, this occasion represented almost an apotheosis of the famed Master of Ceremonies, at which he was represented not only in paint but also in fireworks, prints, poetry and song. Often called 'larger-than-life', at his Benefit that is how he was depicted, fifteen metres tall.

The comic singer W.H. 'Billy' Williams, who performed regularly at Vauxhall between 1823 and 1836, was widely famed for a song of 1833 in honour of Simpson, entitled 'What Think you of Simpson the Beau?'—an 'Historical Comical Comic Ballad', written by Captain Stone, composed by J. Blewitt,[11] and 'Dedicated to the Count de Grasse by Col. Bolsover of the Horse Marines.' The only complete copy I have found is in the Shaw Collection at Harvard,[12] and I transcribe it here in full, not because of any inherent quality, but because it is not otherwise easily obtainable, even online. Apart from taking up the joke of Simpson being Vauxhall's great 'bower', this rather poor song includes several biographical details about Simpson, including that he was only four feet seven inches (1.4m) high, although, to be fair, this does refer to the time when he was only a boy in the navy so he may have gained some height afterwards. He was, though, known to be shorter than average, and slightly overweight.

FIG.9   Simpson and a dolorous lamplighter ascending in a balloon.
'This night Vauxhall will close forever' by Laman Blanchard.
From George Cruikshank's 'Omnibus' (1842), p.175. Private collection.

1. What think you of Simpson the beau?
Who at Vauxhall was always the go
He's an elegant Man, For a Lady with a fan
Or a Dandy who sues for a Box.

Chorus: Off he goes on his toes
With his pretty black Cloaths
Lord! how vain of his Cane!
See he's coming again
What think you of Simpson the beau? O
O what think you of Simpson the beau?

2. For thirty six years he's been Chief
Inspector of Fowls Ham and Beef
Besides he's the knack
As grand taster of rack
To infuse all with spirits around
Off he goes . . .

3. To the Noble, accomplish'd, sweet Ladies
Who prized this Lothario in gay days
To the Princes of blood
Even those 'fore the flood
He offers his very best bow
Off he goes . . .

4. He blesses the worthy Proprietors
Bows, flatters, and quiets e'en rioters
And tho' he looks sable
To Cane he's quite able
All those who stick up for a fight.
Off he goes . . .

5. With RODNEY he kicked up a row
Which his friends of the mess must allow
He swears by the mass
That he nibbled long Grasse

What a Nebuchadnezzar was he
Off he goes . . .

6. This Monster was five feet eleven
Brave SIMPSON just four feet & seven
How horrid the fight
From morn until night
Which raised mighty SIMPSON to Glory
Off he goes . . .

7. To Music he moves quite Stick-ato
In toe toe you'll find him legato
Though he's not such a Flat
But he knows what he's at
For his key has been ever C. Sharp
Off he goes . . .

8. Even Artists their time to beguile
Have Painted brave SIMPSON in Oil
And by aid of the lamp
Given nature a stamp
And raised him just thirty feet high
Off he goes . . .

9. To stand high is the wish of us all
But SIMPSON you're growing too tall
Indeed such devices
Are worthy high prices
And not to be treated so light
Off he goes . . .

11. Vauxhall hath its bowers and flowers
Its Rockets, and shelters from showers –
But SIMPSON away
All would fall to decay –
For he's surely the gardens–best bower
Off he goes . . .

12. God bless all his friends and his backers,
And those who exalt him in Crackers
Tho' burning the shame
It raises his fame
So adieu to this wonderful Star

Off he goes see his toes
Lord he's sing'd his black Cloaths
All in pain for his Cane!
We shan't see it again
What think you of SIMPSON the beau?

Verse 6 of this song refers to the massive portrait of Simpson, thirty feet high and illuminated with lamps. This was the figure, possibly painted by E.W. Cocks, director of the scene-painting department at Vauxhall, that appears in the background of the engraving showing Simpson welcoming the Duke of Wellington to his benefit night on 19 August 1833 (*see Fig.3*). For this very special occasion, portraits of Simpson were an integral part of the decorations—not only this static illuminated figure behind the Orchestra, but also an even larger figure, forty-five feet (nearly 14m) high, in fireworks, designed by the Vauxhall pyrotechnician Joseph Southby to mechanically bow like Simpson himself; on the same occasion, according to *The Times* (20 August 1833), 'thirty-five landscape illustrations of the splendid Simpson, graced the quadrangle of the Royal Gardens', judging by their number, these must have decorated (temporarily) the remaining supper-boxes to the north and south of the central quadrangle or 'Grove', in place of the old-fashioned paintings by Francis Hayman.

Although Simpson was the only individual, up to that time, granted a Benefit Night by the proprietors, and despite his fame and popularity, it was not the overwhelming success that it should have been, partly because of the weather, which threatened rain. The Benefit was originally intended to mark Simpson's retirement from Vauxhall—an event almost as unthinkable as the ravens retiring from the Tower of London. In the event, however, Simpson preferred not to retire, but returned the following season, and the one after that. The total take for Simpson's 1833 Benefit Night was £2,572; with tickets costing four shillings (the usual price of admission at that period), this suggests that over 12,000 visitors attended—a huge number in view of the unfavourable weather. Ticket no.1,609 is preserved in the Peter Jackson Collection.[13] Because the weather had been against them, the proprietors gave Simpson a second benefit night on 21 July the following year, with special performances by some of the greatest musicians and singers of the day—Madame Pasta, Madame Gandolfi (or Grandolfi), Signor de Begnis and Niccolo Paganini all performed for it without a fee.[14] Together, these two occasions would have allowed Simpson to retire in comfort, but he chose to continue his duties until his death in 1835, presumably relishing the celebrity and status it gave him.

To honour his remarkable talents and qualities, in 1834 the proprietors commissioned a plaster bust of Simpson from Lewis Brucciani, of 5 Little Russell Street, to be placed in the Saloon. This bust does not appear in any of the visual documentation, and there is no sign of it thereafter—its present whereabouts are unknown; it may eventually have been included amongst the 'Busts of Eminent Men' sold by Drivers on 29 August 1859. At the earlier Drivers sale on the premises on 12 October 1841, 'four busts of the celebrated Simpson' (lot 142) were sold for ten shillings; these may have been small versions of Brucciani's original, intended for sale to the public.

A FINAL EPISODE in Simpson's career does nothing to dilute the character of his M.C., and was one of the most newsworthy. In 1833, he announced his intention of ascending in Charles Green's gas balloon. He was clearly nervous when the day came—'his whole person shaking like the skeleton of Jerry Abershaw in a high wind'[15]—but he was fortunately prevented from risking his neck by 'a thousand amiable, interesting, and beautiful females' who rushed forward to stop him going; or, depending on which explanation you prefer, by a certain Mr Cave, who offered twenty-five guineas to go up in his place, or even, less credibly, by a group of English aristocrats who thought it undignified for Simpson to ascend in a balloon. For this occasion he had exchanged his usual sober attire for something rather more colourful; 'rose-coloured inexpressibles [breeches], silk stockings, and jacket of ethereal blue, with a splendid yellow dahlia (or dandelion) in his button-hole.' He had already removed his 'shallow of green satin (a low-crowned hat, tapering down to the wide curled brim),

FIG.10 A Mournful Simpson at the close of what might have been the last night of Vauxhall, with a verse loosely based on a passage from Shakespeare's *Tempest* (Act IV, Sc.1): 'The cloud-capp'd Towers, the gorgeous Palaces.' *From George Cruikshank's 'Omnibus' (1842), p.176. Private collection.*

decorated with purple ostrich feathers'.[16] So Simpson did, at least once, wear a different costume, but this one must have been equally, or even more flamboyant than his usual uniform. On the occasion of his re-assumption of his duties on the opening night of his final year, 1835,[17] Simpson appears to let his standards drop one more time, and to have made himself indistinguishable from other men in the crowd, maybe to reveal something of the real man, maybe just to give journalists something to write about. He is described in a press report of 19 May 1835 as 'not in his usual costume... but, as much interest will be felt about his appearance, we think it right to state that he wore an undress black coat, light waistcoat, and fawn-coloured continuations [trousers]; his hair was unpowdered, and his hat was of smaller dimensions than that which last season formed so prominent a feature in the attractions of the gardens.'

It was on Christmas Day 1835, well outside the Vauxhall season, that C.H. Simpson died at his home, 31 Holywell Street, Strand (where he had lived for at least five years), aged just sixty-five, childless and unmarried. He was buried at St John the Evangelist, Westminster, on 31 December, almost within sight of Vauxhall Gardens across the river. I know of only one surviving relic of Simpson—his 1808 oval ivory staff-pass to Vauxhall Gardens is preserved at the British Museum, in the Montague Guest Collection.[18]

Following Simpson's demise, one of the Vauxhall's waiters, 'Little' John Lewis smartened himself up, started using Rowland's kalydor (a hair oil), wore whiter and more starched cravats, and exchanged his 'rudely carved pantaloons and gaiters' for 'the Nugee coat and a pair of O'Shaughnessy pumps', all in the hope of sliding seamlessly into Simpson's place. But Lewis was not the proprietors' choice, and a certain Edward Fisher Longshawe is recorded on handbills of 1836 as the new M.C. After six years, during which several professional actors took on the role, the job was offered to Henry Widdicomb (1813–1868), still Circus Master of Astley's Amphitheatre. Widdicomb, who had himself appeared in pantomime when young, held down the two jobs simultaneously, suggesting that neither venue was a full-time commitment for him, as it had been for his illustrious predecessor.

Simpson's ghost was evoked by cartoonists (*Figs.9 and 10*), poets and songsters writing of Vauxhall; the famous silhouette continued to be used for political satire (*Fig.11*), and the man himself was long remembered by Vauxhall's regulars. Theodosius Purland wrote to his friend John Fillinham, on the occasion of the final closure of the gardens, on 25 July 1859, 'we will drink to the immortal memory of Jonathan Tyers – Hogarth and Simpson! Yes we will do all that befits us to do on the melancholy occasion.'[19]

To many people, Simpson was Vauxhall, as Vauxhall was Simpson – to continue to open the Gardens after his death was meaningless madness; nobody could take his place. Without his greeting and his obsequious letters, Vauxhall was nothing. Indeed, only five years after Simpson died, the proprietors were declared bankrupt, and the Gardens were closed for a whole season. A series of different lessees took on the venue, but none could make it pay, and the Gardens inevitably closed for ever in 1859 after a fitful final two decades.

Simpson's celebrity was such that he was included in the works of W.M. Thackeray, of Charles Dickens, and of several historians of nineteenth-century London. Even today, Simpson is remembered in Vauxhall – Simpson House, the biggest and most prominent apartment block on the 1930s Vauxhall Gardens Estate, overlooking the site of the pleasure garden, is named after him, an honour he shares with several of the better-known singers of his day.

FIG.11 A caricature, after John Doyle, of Henry Peter Brougham, 1st Baron Brougham and Vaux (1778–1868), Whig Lord Chancellor of England from 1830 to 1834. Brougham was famed for his objectionable personality and his love of ceremonial costume. His speech bubble contains the words 'Sir Herbert — / "Welcome to the Royal property".' The English Judge, and Principal of the Arches Sir Herbert Jenner (1778–1852) was appointed to the Privy Council in 1834. Doyle made frequent use of Vauxhall's performers and personalities in his satirical political cartoons, especially of Lord Vaux, and Simpson was, of course, an irresistible model. *Ducôte & Stephens after 'H.B.' [John Doyle], 'The New Vaux-Hall Master of the unCeremoniesous! Poor Simpson eclipsed!' (1834). Lithograph.* CVRC 0636.

THE SURPRISING CAREER OF C.H. SIMPSON

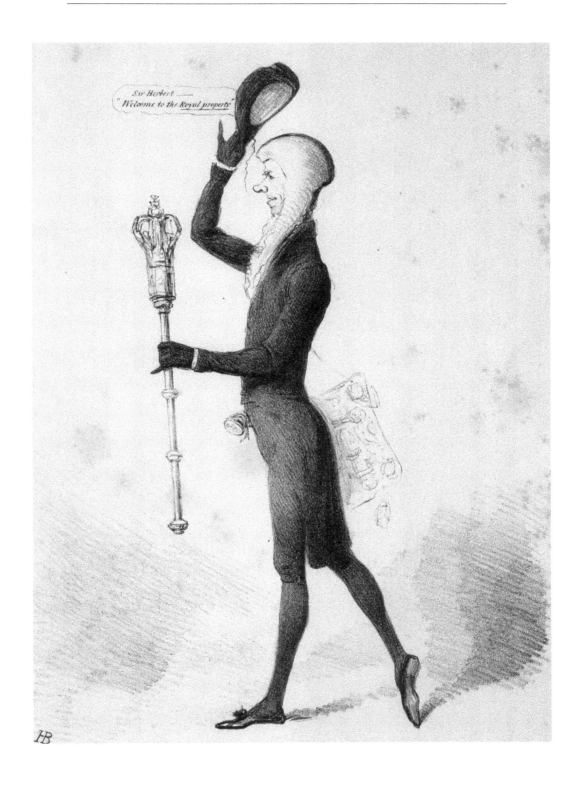

VAUXHALL GARDENS in contemporary *CHILDREN'S BOARD GAMES*

I N 2019 I attended a lecture intriguingly entitled 'The Shows and Sights of Georgian London – a Board Game tour of the Metropolis' by Professor Adrian Seville at the Society of Antiquaries in Burlington House. Professor Seville is a leading authority on English board games and has created what must be the finest collection of historic board games in the UK, so the talk promised to be interesting and wide-ranging.[20]

I had heard a rumour that Vauxhall Gardens, the great pleasure garden of Georgian London, made an appearance on children's board games in the nineteenth century, so I was planning to ask the speaker whether he had come across this in his collecting. But the lecturer soon pre-empted my question, and Vauxhall Gardens turned up with some regularity throughout his talk, much to my surprise. Vauxhall was the only one of the pleasure gardens to occur in this context, but it did occur, and frequently.

It is clear that Vauxhall Gardens, which did not close until 1859, was so familiar to everybody that its use in this context was unremarkable. Its commonly-held reputation today as a notorious place of low morals

---

FIG.1 Handbill for the Vauxhall Juvenile Fete of 2 July 1849. CVRC 0699.

ROYAL GARDENS, VAUXHALL,

OPEN EVERY EVENING DURING THE WEEK, (Saturday excepted).

The Proprietors respectfully inform the Nobility, Gentry, and Public, that,

On MONDAY, JULY 2nd.

WILL BE GIVEN

A GRAND JUVENILE FETE!!

WITH

IMMENSE ATTRACTIONS.

ROTUNDA THEATRE.
Scenes in the Circle by the celebrated

MASTER HERNANDEZ!
Acknowledged to be the Greatest Wonder of his Art; and

Mons. AURIOLS'
UNRIVALLED TROUPE OF FRENCH EQUESTRIANS.

The FIREWORKS by Mr. Darby,
On an extra scale of Brilliancy and Splendour.

THE ILLUMINATIONS consist of **100,000** EXTRA LAMPS!

A delightful View of the LAGO MAGGIORE!! A MOONLIGHT View of the City of MOULTAN, by Roberts. A FAIRY LAKE and GROTTO, by Meadows.

THE ITALIAN WALK!
Which has been considerably extended and improved, with its stately Trees, Statuary, and Fountains, is now open to the Public, giving a Promenade half-a-mile in length.

An American Bowling Saloon is now Open,
With all the American Drinks prepared entirely by Americans.
Adjoining is the **Archery Ground**, Brilliantly Illuminated.

The **Pictorial Embellishments, &c.,** consist of highly picturesque and Panoramic Views on the Rhine, Painted on 2,000 feet of canvas, by F. G. Day, Artist. The CELEBRATED NEPTUNE!! is now completely restored. The MYSTERIOUS ZADOC will be found at his Eastern Temple. Near this spot has been constructed an excellent SHOOTING GALLERY.

The Supper Pavilion!! This magnificent Saloon has been beautified and re-decorated. The **Refreshments, of the First Quality,** including Tea and Coffee, will be supplied at moderate charges. The **Wines** from the highly respectable firm of Messrs. LAWFORD & MAITLAND, 12, George Yard, City.

THE GRAND SALLE DE DANSE!! conducted by Mr. MOXSY, 120 feet in length, and 50 feet in width, tastefully re-decorated and improved. **LA DANSE AL FRESCO** under the superintendence of Mr. A. LEONARD.

ADMISSION, 2s. 6d. **CHILDREN HALF-PRICE.**
KEMSHEAD, Printer,] **No Extra Charge.** [Lambeth.

was, in the early nineteenth century, sufficiently forgotten to allow its uncontroversial inclusion in a game for children. The closely-crafted atmosphere of Vauxhall Gardens at that time, as indeed throughout its life as a pleasure garden, was one of what American theme park designers would later call 'safe danger'. Children were taken to Vauxhall by their parents throughout its history, and in the nineteenth century some of its most successful events were to be the so-called Juvenile Fetes, introduced for a younger audience by the new lessees, Frederick Gye and Thomas Bish, in 1821, and held regularly thereafter (*Fig.1*).

Early board games, marketed for this same audience, were printed on paper supported on a linen base and often folded for storage into a pouch or slip-case, much like road maps of the twentieth century. They were usually 'race' games, in which the winner was the first to land on the final square after surviving several set-backs. The twentieth-century equivalent would be something like Snakes and Ladders, in which players can be made to go back, or pay forfeits, as well as forward, depending on where they land. Nineteenth-century games often included a long set of instructions, detailing what to do if a player landed on particular squares. More often than not, players would be keen to avoid the Vauxhall Gardens square on the board, because if you landed there you would have to spend two turns enjoying the entertainments, or else you would have your pocket picked and lose all your counters—'safe danger' could hardly be better illustrated.

Race games formed part of a long tradition going back at least to the later sixteenth century, when the first printed games were published and sold. Although these games are known to have been printed since the 1580s, the earliest known printed board game in Britain, called 'The Game of the Goose', was first recorded on its entry at Stationers Hall in June 1597. Board games are always rare survivals because they were so well used by their young owners and would be disposed of once they looked worn and dirty, to be replaced by something newer and more exciting.

Traditional dice were not normally used in playing these board games; this was because of their association with gambling and also because of the consequent heavy taxation imposed on their sale. This prompted the reintroduction of a toy called a teetotum, a small spinning top that was often prescribed as a dice-substitute for use with children's board games (*see Fig.3*).

FIG. 2 The central oval from the board game 'The New & Favorite Game of Mother Goose and the Golden Egg', showing Mother Goose in flight. CVRC 0721.

FIG. 3 Teetotum made of bone, from around 1800. CVRC 0726.

These teetotums could be hand-made at home, so were a useful tax-free substitute for dice. Some are very attractive small objects in their own right. In use, they are significantly quieter than dice, so may have recommended themselves to parents for that reason as well. Two twentieth-century games continued to employ teetotums—one a cricket game called 'Owzatt!' and the other a gambling game called 'Put-and-Take', both of which I knew in my own childhood in the 1950s.

The earliest game mentioned in Professor Seville's talk in which Vauxhall Gardens played a part was called 'The New & Favorite Game of Mother Goose and the Golden Egg', first designed and published in 1808 by John Wallis Sr. of 13 Warwick Square, and retailed by his son John Wallis Jr. of 188 Strand, London. This was produced as a hand-coloured etching on paper backed onto linen and folded into a card pouch. A fine example of this game is in Professor Seville's collection, and another, less well preserved (*see Figs. 2, 8*), has recently entered my own Vauxhall Gardens collection from the dealership of Tony Mulholland in Sussex, whose catalogue notes have provided some of the description I have used in this essay.

THE SOURCE FOR the idea behind this version of the game of Mother Goose is not hard to discover. In autumn 1806 the 35-year-old Thomas John Dibdin was approached by Thomas Harris, manager of the Covent Garden Theatre, to write a Christmas pantomime. Thomas Dibdin had been something of a theatrical jack-of-all-trades, having had some success as an actor, a singer, a songwriter, and even a scene-painter, but his strength lay in writing all sorts of theatrical productions, not least the production of pantomimes. Dismayed at the lack of time to prepare anything for Harris, Dibdin dusted off an old script that had been rejected by the same theatre five years earlier: *Harlequin and Mother Goose, or The Golden Egg*. The comedian and dancer Joseph Grimaldi (1778–1837) was to play the dual role of Squire Bugle and Clown, and other roles were, according to one source, 'given to members of the Bologna family of acrobats'. This was the family of John Peter (or 'Jack') Bologna (1775–1846), brought to England as a boy by his family who had formed a troupe of tumblers. Jack Bologna worked at some of the main London theatres, first at Sadler's Wells in 1792 and later at Covent Garden, specialising in pantomime. There is meant to be a watercolour at the Museum of London by T.M. Grimshaw of one of the performances of Mother Goose in 1808, with Jack Bologna as Colin/Harlequin, Miss Searle as Colinette/Columbine, Joseph Grimaldi as Squire Bugle/Clown, Louis Bologna as Avaro/Pantaloon and Samuel Simmons as Mother Goose; sadly I have been unable to trace this picture.[21]

Thomas Dibdin's pantomime opened at Covent Garden Theatre on 26 December 1806,[22] directed by Charles Farley (who later directed the re-enactments of the Battle of Waterloo at Vauxhall Gardens); Mother Goose was preceded on stage by a version of George Lillo's 1731 tragedy *The London Merchant or the History of George Barnwell*, a piece based on a popular ballad, in which an apprentice is seduced into an association with a vicious prostitute, leading to his eventual execution for theft and murder. This gloomy story left the audience hungry for something to amuse and entertain them, which is exactly what Dibdin and Grimaldi had come up with. After the pantomime's opening scenes of illicit youthful love between Colin and Colinette, and Squire Bugle's cruelty, Mother Goose, portrayed as a benevolent witch, transforms the characters into their pantomime personas; Grimaldi's Squire Bugle becomes the 'Clown', while the young lovers are magically recast as Harlequin and Columbine. A series of scenes of slapstick violence plays out including an episode in Vauxhall Gardens (*Fig.4*); here, the Clown and Pantaloon manage to cheat their way in by disguising themselves as two of the so-called 'Pandean Minstrels', using various domestic utensils—a fish kettle with a ladle and whisk, and a household broom, as noted in the game's instructions.

The Pandeans, who played different sizes of pan-pipes, and various percussion instruments, were a popular group of musicians from southern Europe. They first appeared at Vauxhall, dressed in exotic, quasi-military costume in 1803, gaining huge popularity from the start, especially among female visitors, subsequently reappearing there every season for more than twenty years. The engraving of them by John Lee after E.F. Burney (1806) (*Fig.5*) shows why the Clown chose the disguise he did, and why its success, under comic circumstances, might just have been credible, while the audience could all see through it.

Even though he was not happy with the pantomime himself (partly because of the amount of strenuous work it involved), Grimaldi had found in the Clown his most famous vehicle and he was, finally, after years of supporting roles, a 'star'. The production ran for almost a hundred nights in 1806/7, making the Covent Garden proprietors the unprecedented profit of £20,000. 'The New & Favorite Game of Mother Goose', published as a board game two years later, commemorated one of the most remarkable events in London's theatrical history, and it allowed families to recreate their memories of the pantomime in the comfort of their own homes. Other printed items of the time inspired by the pantomime, including illustrated writing sheets, proved equally popular.

Dibdin's pantomime strongly recalled the long tradition of the *commedia dell'arte*, in which Harlequin and Columbine played regular parts, but it also prefigured later pantomimes based on fairy stories with fantastic and magical characters in mythical settings. Dibdin's original work has been adapted and altered many times since it was first written; the story of Mother Goose has come down to us in many forms, often quite different from the pantomime. Perrault's moralising fairy tales, translated into English in a publication of 1729, popularised the name, but the fame and spread of the story appear to derive almost entirely from the success of Dibdin's pantomime, leading to the adoption of Mother Goose as a purely English figure.

AFTER THE FIRST of the really popular board games, others soon followed, several with London themes, and with names like 'The Panorama of London' (published by John Harris 1809). Square 30 is Vauxhall Gardens, where the player has to 'pay [with some of his counters] to hear the music and singing'. 'The Survey of London', by William Danton, was published in 1820. This had several well-produced views of London sights, with moral captions to most illustrations. The game 'Scenes in London', published by Edward Wallis (younger son of John Wallis Sr.), in 1825, included the Cosmorama,[23] the Monument and the British Museum, among several other sights. Square 16 is Vauxhall Gardens, where the player has his pocket picked, so losing all the counters he has left. The Vauxhall illustration shows a night-time crowd in front of the illuminated Orchestra, with glowing tableaux of moons, stars and festoons. 'London Sights, or All Round St. Paul's, a new and amusing game' was printed on a cotton handkerchief, possibly as a souvenir for visitors to the Great Exhibition of 1851. A nice example of

FIG.4 Square 19 from 'The New & Favorite Game of Mother Goose and the Golden Egg', showing the episode at Vauxhall; at the lower right are the two figures disguised as Pandean minstrels, standing in front of the Orchestra.

FIG.5   Pandean Minstrels, in Performance at Vaux-Hall. *John Lee after Edward Francis Burney (1806). Etching.* CVRC 0176.

this has been acquired by the Foundling Museum in Brunswick Square, London because the twelfth space shows the Foundling Hospital as one of the great tourist sights of London (*Fig.6*). Of course, Vauxhall is there too, as square no. 40 (*Fig.7*).

This game, incidentally, is one of the few where to land on Vauxhall was actually a good thing, because you were instructed to move forward four squares to Wylde's Globe, an attraction that ran only from 1851 to 1856, so giving a tight date bracket within which the undated game must have been produced.

WHEN THE NEW and Favorite Game of Mother Goose and the Golden Egg arrived in my collection, it was pretty fragile, stained with some unidentified brown splashes, and in a tired state generally. It had also, unsurprisingly, lost its original slip-case. However, it was otherwise remarkably complete, and its 'Vauxhall Gardens' square (the reason I acquired it) was clear and colourful, despite being split in two by one of the folds of the game. This uncommon survival was a good case for careful conservation treatment, but, because of its mixed materials and its fragility, it would need a real expert. Somebody I had worked with before was paper conservator Pamela Allen; Pam and her husband Stephen are both expert paper conservators, and Stephen has archive experience too, including book conservation and lining paper onto linen backings; Stephen also has previous experience of a similar board game of the same period, so their combined skills and long experience were invaluable. The game was passed to them in October 2019 and returned to me three months later (*Fig.8*).

The conservation process raised several points of interest about this game which would not otherwise have come to light, and which may be otherwise unknown. First, running vertically through the first square of the game, the paper has an incomplete watermark 'JOHN DICKINSON & CO. 1810', showing that this impression of the game was printed at least two years after the plate was made, and on a paper of high quality. It is not known how many impressions of individual games would have been produced, or indeed how long they were produced for, but it would take several hundred sales to justify the initial outlay and production costs.

It soon became apparent to the conservators that the spiral of the game itself was printed (by the intaglio process)[24] on different paper stock (the one with the watermark) to the letterpress instructions at the bottom of the game. The paper for the 'game' area is a 'laid' paper (showing the mesh marks of the manufacturing process), thinner and smoother than the letterpress 'instructions' paper; it is also very strong; the instructions are printed on a slightly heavier hand-made 'wove' paper, with no watermark. The odd aspect of this is that it was normal practice for etchings and engravings (intaglio prints) to be printed on a soft, sized paper that could be moistened, and would easily collect the ink from the engraved lines. This means that the printer of the game area, Thomas Sorrell, of 86 Bartholomew Close, London, was highly skilled and took considerable time and effort over the project. It might also suggest that Dickinson's new fine laid paper was not entirely suitable for the relief process of letterpress.

The 1810 date of the watermark corresponds to the time that Dickinson's mill installed a state-of-the-art paper-making machine; the watermark itself is of a standard type for handmade paper, although it could easily have been incorporated into a machine-made product too. John Dickinson's company, founded in 1804 in Hertfordshire, became a significant player in the stationery industry in England. By 1809, he had already patented a new process for making continuous sheets of paper at his Nash Mills in Apsley. Previously, only single sheets of limited size could be made, but Dickinson's process began to produce extended lengths on his 'endless web' machine, in fact a revolving cylinder of mesh, onto which the pulp was drawn before being finished under a dandy-roller which also produced the watermark. Dickinson specialised in manufacturing fine and lightweight but robust paper. Because of its size, and its combination of thinness and strength, Dickinson's paper would have been ideal for use in John Wallis's new folding board game. What is obvious is that the production process which mounted the paper onto its linen backing must have been quite sophisticated, probably using new static steam presses. Linen and paper react quite differently to drying out from any wet-glueing process, which is likely to lead to the structure curling, as the conservators found when they tried to reinforce the paper sections after removal from the linen, even with very fine backings, before remounting them onto linen—a standard type of intervention for preserving old paper, but one that had to be abandoned in this case because, without the intervention of

VAUXHALL GARDENS IN BOARD GAMES

FIG.6 The London Sights game printed on a cotton handkerchief, c.1851.
Courtesy of the Foundling Museum.

FIG.7 Detail of the Vauxhall Orchestra.

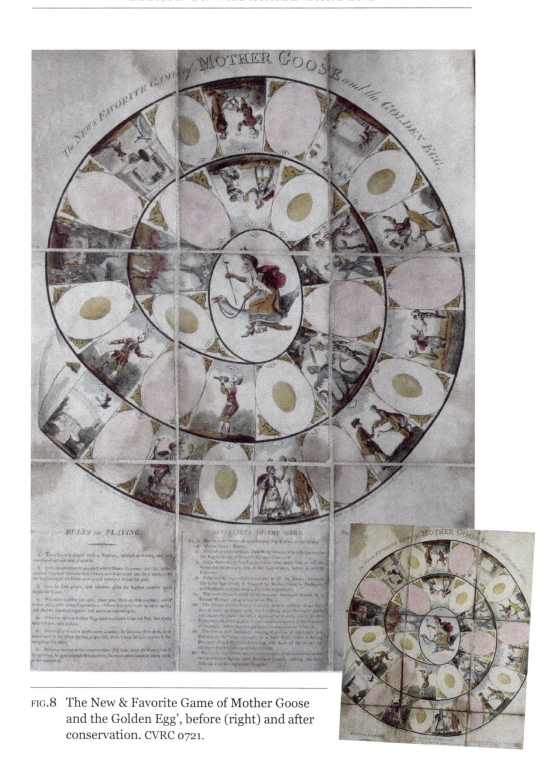

FIG.8 The New & Favorite Game of Mother Goose and the Golden Egg', before (right) and after conservation. CVRC 0721.

a steam-press, it was distorting the sections of the game. The original linen backing was not reused for the conserved paper sections, partly because it was too damaged and retained some of the contaminants that had damaged the paper surface, and partly because the original had been in two pieces roughly sewn together in the middle of the game area, putting unnecessary stress on the paper; a full sheet of clean nineteenth-century linen was sourced by the Allens for the replacement, retaining the characteristic colour and texture of the original.

Stephen Allen, the conservator, said to me after the work was completed, 'We have spent more time thinking and planning this conservation project than physically doing any work,' but the work was certainly done, and the game is now much more presentable. More importantly, is in the best possible condition to survive for another two centuries, as long as it can avoid being played on by children who spill their hot chocolate (or worse) over it.

EVANION
THE 'ROYAL CONJUROR'
Supplier of Refreshments to Vauxhall
and OBSESSIVE COLLECTOR
of ENTERTAINMENT EPHEMERA

VANION'S VAST AND wide-ranging collection of playbills, prints, advertisements and other ephemera associated with the Victorian entertainment scene in England is well known; the bulk of it was purchased by the British Museum in 1895, but other museums, libraries and private collections across the world hold large numbers of further items from it.

This Evanion discovery, which throws new light on Evanion's family and his collecting, consists of a pencil signature on the back of a Vauxhall Gardens handbill advertising the 'Royal Fete' on 21 August 1833 (*Figs.2, 3*) and a brief autobiographical note in the same hand scribbled in pencil on the reverse of another handbill, this one advertising a concert series in 1831 (*Figs.4, 5*).

The signature reads 'H. Evanion 1872'; the significance of the date is unclear, although the official change of his surname from Evans to Evanion had only recently taken place, so he may just have been trying out his new signature (*Fig.3*).

The autobiographical note on the back of the 1831 handbill is less easy to decipher, but has now been transcribed as follows (*Fig.5*):

I was Connected with / Vaux' Gardens from / 1840 to 59 / Also my Grandfather & / Father. / H. Evanion Collection / of Bills, Prints,

FIG.1 M. [Monsieur] Evanion, Royal Conjuror and humourist (1870). *Poster.* © *The British Library Board. Shelfmark: Evan.2589.*

Letters, / Letterpress, remarks, posters / and Advertisements /
Continued to collect 1846 / up to 1888 5 Collections / the Best sold
to Mr. Muset / 1888.

The writing of 'Mr Muset' is obscured, so the reading of this name may
be wrong.

The autobiographical note, brief as it is, gives several new facts
about Evanion. First, it states that his father and grandfather were both
involved at Vauxhall Gardens; second, it affirms that his collection began
seriously in 1846, when he was just fourteen years old, and, finally, that
he sold many of his best items to an unidentified 'Mr. Muset' in 1888.
Evanion would have considered his 'best' items to be those most closely
related to conjuring and magic, especially those with illustrations.
Vauxhall letterpress handbills of the 1830s and 1840s would not have
been highly valued even by Evanion, although today many of them are
vanishingly rare or even precious unique survivals.

It is likely that the mysterious buyer 'Mr. Muset' mentioned in
Evanion's note was the 'wealthy collector in Paris' who bought the part
of Evanion's collection previously seen by H.H. Montgomery, the cleric
and historian.[25] From the available evidence it appears that this was at
least part of the collection that was later acquired in France by Robert
Gould Shaw and presented by him in 1915, bound into nine elegant
volumes, to the Theatre Collection at Harvard University, of which
Shaw himself was the first curator.[26]

Both items with the Evanion manuscript on the back were acquired
as part of a group of ten Vauxhall Gardens handbills, at the estate sale
of the collector Stephen O. Saxe, of White Plains, New York by
an American collector and have since been repatriated to the UK.
It is possible that other items in the group derive from Evanion's
collection, but the only evidence for this would be their unusually
fine condition. Stephen O. Saxe (1930–2019) had been a set designer
for stage and television, but on his retirement in 1985, his abiding
interest in nineteenth-century typography and printing was allowed
free rein, leading to published books and articles, to the founding of

---

FIG.2   Handbill for a 'Royal Fete' at Vauxhall Gardens in 1833. CVRC 0832.
FIG.3   Evanion's signature on the reverse of the handbill. The significance of
the date '1872' is unclear.

UNDER THE ESPECIAL PATRONAGE OF HIS MAJESTY,

ROYAL GARDENS, VAUXHALL.

THE GRANDEST NIGHT
OF THE SEASON,

WEDNESDAY, 21st of AUGUST.

THE NATAL DAY OF HIS MAJESTY WILL BE CELEBRATED BY A

ROYAL FETE
IN HONOR OF OUR BELOVED MONARCH,

THE ROYAL AND MUNIFICENT PATRON OF THESE GARDENS.

In executing the most pleasing Duty of their Season, the Proprietors have to state, that this Gala will be in every respect worthy of the Anniversary it commemorates, and that the arrangements in all the Departments are completing on a greatly extended Scale.

THE ILLUMINATIONS

Will be of the most superb character, particularly a Colossal Piece of surpassing Splendor, constructed entirely for this Night, with upwards of 8,000 Lamps of various colors and sizes: it represents the rich Imperial Crown of Great Britain, prepared, by command of His Majesty, George IV. by Messrs. Rundell and Bridge, for the Coronation.

THE GARDENS

Will be beautifully and emblematically decorated; splendor will reign triumphant, and more than 30,000 additional Lamps will be disposed in the Quadrangle, &c., in various appropriate Devices.

THE MUSIC

Will be also in unison with the occasion, interspersed with an uninterrupted succession of FAVORITE COMIC SONGS AND GLEES.

THE GIGANTIC FIGURE OF MR. SIMPSON

In variegated Lamps, 45 Feet high, will be exhibited on this occasion.

THE FIRE WORKS

Will, as they always do on the King's Birth Day, […] of any other Night, the Artist being paid a large Sum extra. The Figure of […]

DOORS OPEN AT […]

☞ THE GARDENS […]

BALNE, PRINTER, GRACECHURCH STREET.

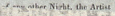

Royal Gardens, Vauxhall.

MONDAY, WEDNESDAY, & FRIDAY

Will be presented a variety of Amusements, including

A CONCERT

OF VOCAL AND INSTRUMENTAL MUSIC,

IN THE OPEN ORCHESTRA.

The New Music composed by Mr. H. R. BISHOP.

Leader, Mr. R. HUGHES.

ACT I.

OVERTURE		Bishop.
GLEE	Messrs. Robinson, Hobbs, and Bedford	The Shamrock, Thistle, and Rose
SONG*	Miss Martin	The Lad in the Jacket of Blue
SONG	Mr. Robinson	Heart's Ease
COMIC TRIO	Miss Hughes, Messrs. G. Stansbury & Bedford	Vadasi via di qua
SONG*	Mrs. Mapleson	With my Bow and my Horn
SONG*	Mr. Hobbs	The Beam of Beauty's Eye

The celebrated MICHEL BOAI, the CHIN MELODIST, will play a March, with Variations.

SONG*	Miss George	The Indian Girl's Song
COMIC GLEE	Messrs. Robinson, Hobbs, G. Stansbury & Bedford	Old King Cole
COMIC SONG	Mr. W. H. Williams	Thinking
FINALE (Tutti)		The Halt of the Caravan

Between the Acts of the Concert, the Promenade will be enlivened by Bands of Music, and JOEL, the ALTONIAN SIFFLEUR, will give his Imitations of various Birds.

Under the Gallery of the Rotunda will be exhibited, from Ten till Twelve, the following Views:

The Great Fountain in the Garden of Nithelmshohe, near Cashel;
The Imperial Palace of St. Petersburgh, near the Neva;
Madrid from the Road to Segovia;
Ansicht, on the Praga;—The grand Square and Cathedral, Mexico;
Optical Illusions, &c.

At the extremities of the Quadrangle are several extensive Views, by COCKS; including

The Eruption of Vesuvins in 1794, from a Picture recently received from Naples;
Two large Dioramic Pictures of the Liverpool and Manchester Rail Road, from Drawings taken on the spot, &c.
A grand View of Brighton, 40 feet wide, taken purposely for Vauxhall, by COCKS, will be seen from the Rotunda;
An entirely new Rural Scene, by Moonlight, with real Water-mill at work, &c.

ACT II.

OVERTURE		Bishop.
SONG*	Mr. Robinson	The Bloom is on the Rye
SONG	Miss George	Not To-Night
SONG	Mr. Williams	The King of the O-Y-Ees
SONG	Miss Hughes	The Spanish Girl
GLEE	Messrs. Robinson, Hobbs, Jones, Stansbury, and Bedford	Five merry Boys are we
SONG	Miss Martin	There is a Lad
DUET	Messrs. Hobbs and Bedford	Our merry Ship
SONG	Mrs. Mapleson	The Bride of a Soldier
COMIC SKETCH	Messrs. Robinson, Hobbs, Stansbury, & Bedford	The Little Pigs

MICHEL BOAI will play the Overture to Lodoiska.

COMIC DUET	Miss Martin and Mr. Williams	Mr. Jeremy
FINALE	(Solo and Chorus)	God save the King

*The Music of the Songs, &c. marked * may be had in the Gardens and principal Music Shops.*

AFTER THE CONCERT, A DISPLAY OF

FIRE WORKS,

By the ARTISTS OF THE GARDENS, D'ERNST and SOUTHBY, alternately; with the

WATER SCENE,

Allowed to be the most splendid specimen of scenic effect ever produced.—The Military and Scotch Bands will be in attendance, and play at intervals during the Evening, and immediately after the Fire Works.

DOORS OPEN AT HALF-PAST SEVEN.—ADMISSION, 4s.

Nightly Tickets to be had at 23, Ludgate Hill; 141, Fleet Street; 8, Charing Cross; and 148, Oxford Street.

☞ BOOKS OF THE SONGS TO BE HAD ONLY IN THE GARDENS.

PAINE, Printer, 38, Gracechurch Street.

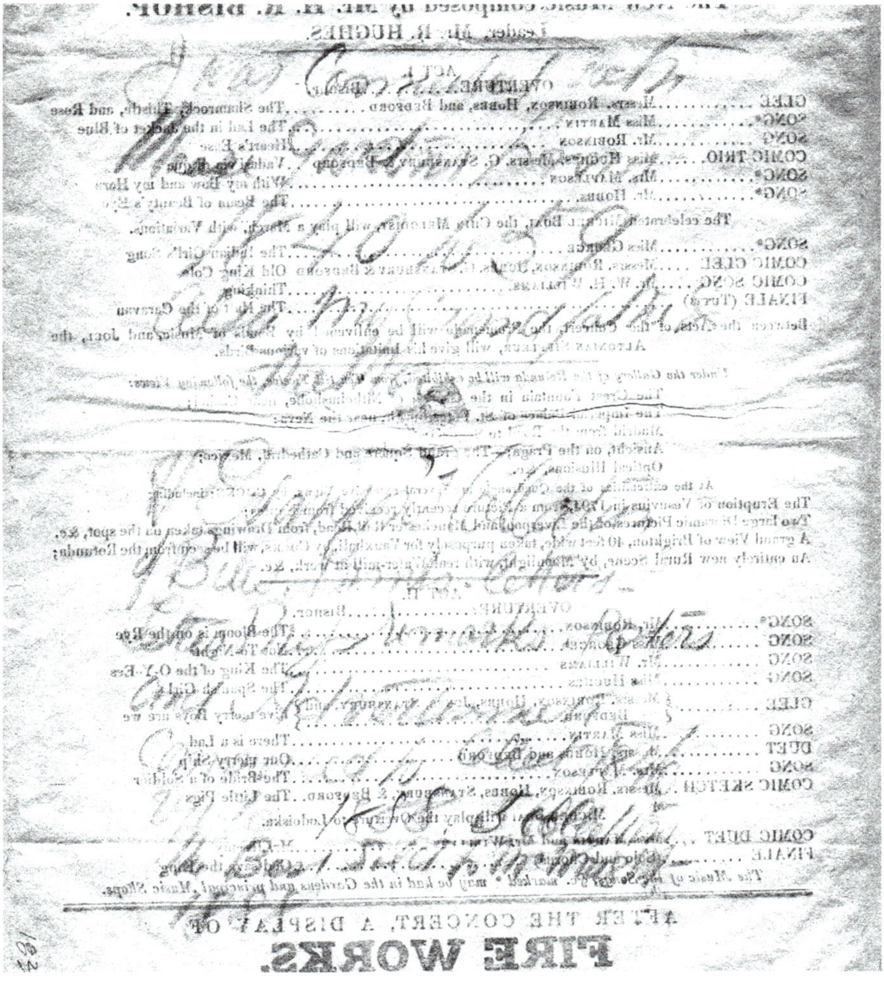

FIG.4 Handbill for an 1831 concert series at Vauxhall Gardens. CVRC 0833.
FIG. 5. Evanion's autobiographical note on the reverse of handbill.

FIG.6 'The Fall of Napoleon' (1837). Detail of a satirical print showing several handbills, including one for a Grand Gala at Vauxhall Gardens (top left) stuck to the wall of the mythical 'Waterloo Tavern' on 'Wellington Street'. *Georg Zobel, after George Augustus Wallis. Mezzotint.* CVRC 0843.

the American Printing History Association (APHA), and to an extensive collection of print samples, typefaces and even presses. His collection, and his encyclopaedic knowledge, were generously and happily shared with many other interested parties. Saxe was too young to have acquired these items directly from Evanion, but from their unusually good state of preservation it is clear that they were in one or more similar but unidentified collections between 1905 and the 1980s; the private collections of Arthur J. Margery (1871–1945) and James B. (Jimmy) Findlay (1904–1973) are both known to have held items from Evanion's collection.[27] Saxe could well have acquired these items in the UK from Findlay's estate.

Most such Vauxhall ephemera have suffered much worse treatment than these pieces because they were cheaply printed on lightweight paper, and then either pinned or pasted on walls or billboards in all weathers, or handed out in the street, and finally thrown away as worthless (*Fig.6*). These handbills were intended to last no more than a few days. The fact that these items from Saxe's collection have lasted almost two hundred years is partly due to the fact that Henry Evans's family was directly involved at Vauxhall Gardens as suppliers of refreshments for at least two generations before Henry was born. The young Evanion is bound to have accompanied his father and grandfather on their delivery trips to the Gardens, and is likely to have picked up handbills himself, or been given them by indulgent members of staff. If he was only eight years old when these visits began in 1840, as stated in his note shown in *Fig.5*, it is likely that this is how his collection began, possibly with an illustrated handbill of something like a balloon ascent by Charles Green, or of one of the famous Vauxhall firework displays, that the boy found lying around in a back room. No value was attributed to such throwaway items once the performance had taken place, so they became so much scrap paper. It is not impossible that Henry's obsession with collecting, as well as his fascination with performance, juggling and sleight of hand were both inspired by Vauxhall's brilliant nineteenth-century spectacle and performers.

HENRY EVANS WAS the eldest son of Thomas (1810–c.1849) and Susan Evans (1810–c.1883), confectioners and victuallers of Kennington Lane. In the 1841 census, Henry is recorded at the age of about ten living with his parents and his brothers Robert (aged eight), James (six) and Thomas (three), at Windmill Row, Upper Kennington Lane, south of the intersection of Kennington Lane and Kennington Road (*Fig.7*). Only seven years later, he had launched his career as a conjuror, illusionist, ventriloquist and juggler; his first professional engagement was at the Rock Inn, Kemp Town, Brighton as a support act to a ventriloquist called Newman and his family. In the same year, he put on a solo show called a 'Soirée Fantastique' at the Town Hall in the small town of Langport in Somerset; he played many such towns and villages around the British Isles during his career.

Since childhood Evans had practiced magic tricks on a makeshift stage in the loft of his family home to audiences of his friends and brothers, before becoming a professional magician, working on his own and with the Newman family. In the 1860s, he performed three times for members of the royal family, at Sandringham and at Marlborough House; amongst his illusions on the noted occasion at Sandringham was 'The Grand Feat of the Globes of Fire, Fish and Birds'.

In the 1850s, Evans started to use the professional name Evan Ion, maybe in tribute to a perceived Welsh ancestry, but later that decade it was clear that his act needed a more exotic headline, so he contracted the name to 'Evanion', at the same time adopting a French accent during his act. His illusions and ventriloquism always included an element of humour, which proved popular with audiences, whether school-children or members of the royal family. A review of an Evanion performance published in *The Morning Advertiser* of 23 December 1873 states that:

> trick followed trick with wonderful rapidity, and a profusion that speaks highly for Mr. Evanion's resources. He is not only a very skilful professor of the art of legerdemain, but he is happy in possessing a rich vein of comic humour, which he infuses largely into his conversation either with the spectators or with the assistant whom he summons from among the spectators and the result is to excite laughter as well as wonder.

Henry later took on the name Evanion as his legal surname.

Evanion's advertising posters not only capitalised on his royal connection, but also made big claims for his act. In one poster now in the British Library, he proclaims, in the manner of a music-hall 'barker',

> Mr Evanion, who, alone, unaided by confederates, and without all the ordinary apparatus, Deceives the Eye, amazes, bewilders, and baffles the keenest observer, will display his truly miraculous Acquirements in Prestidigitation which surpass everything hitherto presented to the Public, in fact exhibiting powers that seem impossible to be achieved by human agency.

A ticket of 1865, also at the British Library, calls his act a 'Wonderful and amusing entertainment... Exhibiting Startling and Extraordinary Illusions, Laughable Ventriloquial effects & Necromantic Feats. Something New under the Sun'.

Whether his act lived up to all these claims is unclear, but he does appear to have had a long career in magic, with some modest success, and was still active, according to his publicity, until his final illness. His income, however, was never sufficient to tempt him to abandon his father's confectionery business at 221 Kennington Road (just north of the junction with Chester Street, now Chester Way).[28] Having said that, it is clear that his fees for an evening's entertainment were of a professional standard. One of Evanion's handbills that must date from the 1880s gives them as either five guineas, three guineas or two guineas for a two-hour evening entertainment for children. The price depended on the selection of illusions and magic to be performed, but all three included 'Distributions of Presents, Programmes &c'. It is known that his drawing room show for adults was charged at ten guineas.[29]

It was probably a similar type of 'Drawing-Room' show that Evanion performed at the Crystal Palace in Sydenham during a series of six shows at the end of 1880, for which he received half the takings at the door, which came to £20 7s. 6d. Later shows at Sydenham, which appears to have been a regular fixture for Evanion, included his 'Extraordinary Flag Illusion' (*see Fig.8*), as well as 'The Japanese Marionette', 'The Mystic Parrot', The 'Fan Fan Enchantment', 'Vulcan's Chain', the 'Extraordinary Experiment of Wireless Telegraphy by Cards' and the 'Japanese Lady's Reception'.[30]

Bookings like the Crystal Palace would no doubt have been highlights in Evanion's career, with long periods of no magic work at all. It is likely that Henry's mother Susan, and then his wife Mary Ann provided most of the family income by running the confectionery business for him while he was happily occupied with his stage-work, whether performing, lecturing or rehearsing, or else researching the history of magic at the British Museum Reading Room, where he spent every spare hour, presumably much to the frustration and irritation of his long-suffering wife. Henry and Mary Ann (*née* Evans) had married in 1865 at St Mark's church, Kennington; there is no record of any children born to the couple. Mary Ann, who was three or four years younger than her husband and may have been related to him, appears initially to have accompanied Henry in his act, being called a ventriloquist in her own right, but the confectionery business would have been a full-time occupation for her from the time when her mother-in-law Susan was no longer able to work; it would therefore have made sense for her to give up performing and to do what she could to support herself and her husband, and to look after the widowed Susan in her old age.

It was already known that T.H. Evans, Evanion's father Thomas Henry Evans, had been a 'Punch-maker for upwards of twenty years to the 'Royal Property" (i.e. The Royal Gardens, Vauxhall). It was also known that 'Henry Evans of Kennington Lane' was supplying 'Ices and Confectionary [*sic*]' to the Gardens in the 1850s,[31] and that a Mr Evans (maybe Evanion himself, or one of his brothers) was, in 1854, helping to staff Vauxhall's Lower Bar, at a salary of £1 1s. per week, and looking after the reserved seats at 15 shillings a week. Thomas Henry Evans the punch-maker had also been the landlord of the

---

FIG.7   Detail from the 'Weekly Dispatch' map of South London (1863), showing the area within which Evanion lived and where his confectionery business was located. Windmill Row is just to the right of the Licenced Victuallers School, with Park Place (unnamed) just over Kennington Lane from it; Pilgrim Street can be seen to the right of the Phoenix Gas Works north of the Oval; Methley Street had not yet been built, but was located in the blank area in the centre right of this image where the large S appears. The confectionery shop was at the top right of the image, by the 'R' of Kennington Road. The site of Vauxhall Gardens can be seen centre left. '*Cassell's Map of London (South sheet)', drawn and engraved by Edward Weller (1863).* CVRC 0517.

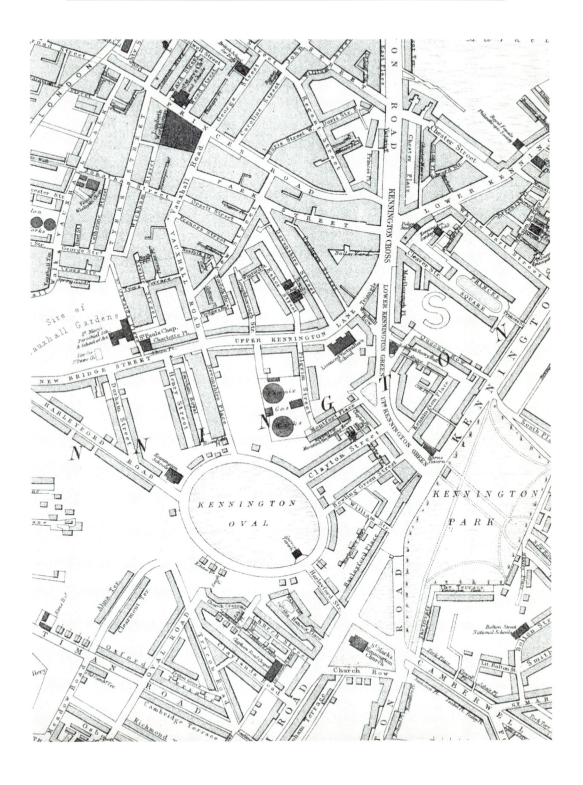

Black Prince public house in Prince's Road, until April 1849; but the 'Henry Evans of Kennington Lane' who supplied ice cream and confectionery must be a reference to Evanion himself and his wife Mary Ann carrying on his parents' trade. Henry had, after all, become a professional pastrycook by the time he was twenty, following in his father's footsteps. Without his family business as a supplier to Vauxhall Gardens, it is likely that Evanion would not have been able to carry on his career in magic.

The role played by Henry's grandfather at Vauxhall, as mentioned in the autobiographical note, is undocumented, but presumably also related to the provision of refreshments from around 1800. In the 1841 census, Thomas and Susan Evans and their four sons were living next door to Thomas and Jane Evans, both aged sixty, and Thomas Sr was described as a fruiterer. These must have been Henry's grandparents, because ten years later, that same Thomas Senior, by now a pastrycook, and his wife Jane were living at 1 Upper Kennington Lane, with Evanion's mother Susan, and three of her sons–the twenty-year-old Henry himself, by now fully qualified as a pastrycook, and his younger brothers Robert and James, aged eighteen and seventeen, probably both at work in the family business. As a fruiterer, Thomas the elder could have supplied Vauxhall Gardens with the oranges and lemons that were usually on the bills of fare, as well as fruit for tarts and pastries, and for the notorious Arrack punch (supplied for two decades by the Evans family) as well. By 1851, Evanion's father, Thomas the younger, disappeared from the records, so had presumably died, which may be the reason why the Black Prince pub needed a new landlord in April 1849. Another ten years on (1861) and the widowed Susan was living with her sons Henry and James (by now a painter and a decorator) at 26 Park Place; this was a curved terrace of houses on the north side of Kennington Lane opposite Windmill Row.[32] Henry's other brother Robert had married and set up his own household by 1860. No trace of Henry's youngest brother Thomas can be found after the 1841 census, when he was just three.

FIG.8 The appearance of Mr. Newman, the original and unrivalled ventriloquist, and Henry Evans Evanion, the Royal illusionist, at the Egham Literary Institute, Surrey. *An illustration of 'Evanion's extraordinary flag illusion' (1874). © The British Library Board. Shelfmark: Evan.2645.*

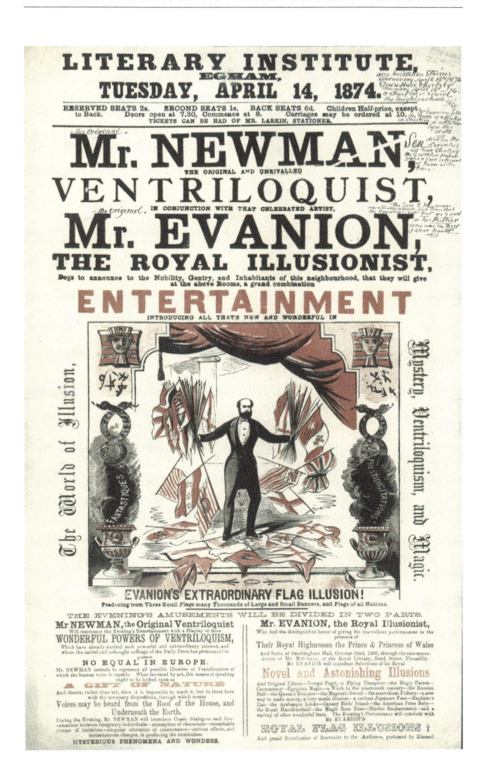

Henry Evans Evanion lived in Kennington all his life, moving several times within a small circuit, from his parents' house on Windmill Row, first to his grandparents' house at 1 Upper Kennington Lane, then with his mother and brother James to Park Place (Kennington Lane), then, following his marriage, to 18 Pilgrim Street, where Montford Place is now, next to the Pilgrim pub (in the 1871 census), then to 22 Kennington Road according to the 1890 Electoral register (*see Fig.7 for locations*); in the 1891 census, Henry and Mary Ann were living at 9 St Anne's Road, where Robert Evans, a widower, was also living with his adult son and daughter; this Robert, described as a 'Theatrical Employee' in the census, must have been Henry's brother; as Robert had lost his wife, and Henry may have been in financial difficulties, it is likely the brothers thought it would make sense for them to share a house. St Anne's Road, between Brixton Road and Clapham Road, just south of The Oval, was renamed Southey Road in 1937; this was the only time Henry's home was marginally outside Kennington's boundary. Henry and Mary Ann had moved to their final home, back in Kennington proper, at 12 Methley Street well before the next census in 1901.

It was at Pilgrim Street in 1871 that we see Henry's legal surname given as 'Evanion' rather than Evans for the first time, much to the confusion of the census-taker, who had to make several attempts at his name. It is also here that his occupation was first given as a 'Professor of Legerdemain' (sleight of hand), and Mary Ann's as a ventriloquist. His mother Susan was still alive, aged about sixty-three, and still at work in the family's confectionery business. In 1871, Henry and Mary Ann had been joined at Pilgrim Street by Charlotte Puris, Henry's sixty-four-year-old aunt, who was a mantle-maker.[33] By the time of the next census, in 1881, Susan has taken Charlotte's place with Henry and Mary Ann, and the family appears to be living over the shop at 221 Kennington Road. Mary Ann herself is by this time being called a confectioner in her own right, suggesting that she was by now running the family business in Susan's place.

The closure of Vauxhall Gardens at the end of the 1859 season must have been a cruel blow to Evanion's family, as they lost their best customer, and an assured source of summer income. Evanion himself would have lost a great source of free material for his collection as well, although he may have been allowed to sort through the scrap paper store before it was used to light the bonfires during the

FIG.9 Henry Evans Evanion in the 1880s. *From Harry Houdini's 'The Unmasking of Robert-Houdin' (1908).*

demolition of the Gardens. In addition, Evanion lost his regular contact with all those clowns, jugglers, mimics, contortionists, ventriloquists, ball-walkers, fortune-tellers, tightrope artists and magicians who performed at Vauxhall in the last three decades of its life. After 1859, though, the confectionery business did survive, first under Susan's care, and then under Mary Ann's; the site of Vauxhall Gardens was built over with houses, schools, pubs and a church, providing many new potential customers, although the new inhabitants were largely in the lower income brackets, so expenditure on luxuries like sweets and pastries would have been strictly limited. There is no doubt that the business suffered, and the several house moves made by Henry and Mary Ann suggest a downward trajectory in their fortunes; it appears that they only narrowly avoided destitution at the Lambeth Workhouse.

In the last year of Evanion's life when he was very ill with cancer and in dire poverty, he met and became a friend of Harry Houdini, who admired Evanion's collection hugely, especially the ephemera associated with the great magicians of the past including Robert-Houdin, Katterfelto, Boaz, Breslaw, Pinetti and others. Houdini purchased many items from Evanion for his own collection, partly in order to support him in his old age, poverty and sickness.[34] Houdini later remembered Evanion as a dear old friend who had introduced him to a vast range of fascinating characters through his collection. Houdini's own collection of ephemera, including numerous items bought from Evanion, is now largely held at the US Library of Congress, and at the University of Texas (Harry Ransom Center).

Evanion also sold a large part of his collection to the British Museum Department of Printed Books (now the British Library) in 1895. This was done in two tranches, on 5 July and 3 October, and amounted to around six thousand items in all. The British Museum curators paid just under £20, in order that the purchase did not have to be reported to the trustees, whose approval was require for acquisitions over £20 and who would have considered the collection beneath their notice or interest. Unfortunately, the money from the British Museum and the apparently paltry sums given by Houdini would not have gone very far to support the couple in their old age.

It is to be hoped that the 'wealthy collector in Paris' was more generous, but this, sadly seems unlikely, for, as Houdini himself tells us, at his first meeting with Evanion, in 1904, when the famous escapologist was on tour in London, Evanion appeared as 'a bent figure, clad in rusty raiment', who the hotel's concierge had not dared send up to Houdini's suite because he appeared so shabby. As a result, Evanion was kept waiting for three hours in the hotel lobby before the two men eventually met. Evanion stood with difficulty and approached Houdini 'with some hesitancy of speech but the loving touch of a collector' as he opened the parcel of 'treasures' he had brought as bait for the great man. The bait worked and Houdini, despite a bout of influenza, rushed over to Evanion's home early the following morning. The two men pored over Evanion's collection and became so deeply engrossed in it that Houdini was missed that evening at the hotel and he had to be dragged away from Evanion's basement home in Methley Street by his brother and his doctor at 3.30 the following morning.

Houdini visited Evanion for the last time at Methley Street, on 7 June 1905, only ten days before his old friend died of throat cancer at St Thomas's Hospital. Methley Street, of course, is now famous as the childhood home (if only briefly) of another entertainer who knew all about severe poverty and deprivation, Charlie Chaplin. When Harry Houdini, on his visits, saw how low Evanion had sunk and how sick he was, the great man quickly set up a fund for his benefit through an advertisement in *The Encore* magazine, donating five pounds himself. All too soon this fund had to pay for Evanion's funeral, with the residue going to his widow, Mary Ann, who survived him by just a few months.

Evanion's chief legacy today is his vast and all-embracing collection of Victorian entertainment ephemera which has been, and continues to be, of inestimable value to scholars and amateurs of the many subjects that it covers. The young Henry Evans and his wife Mary Ann would be staggered that, a century later, single items that he picked up in the back rooms of Vauxhall Gardens for nothing now sell for many times the £20 he received from the British Museum for his entire collection.

The COACH ENTRANCE

New evidence of the popular nostalgia for Vauxhall after it closed

THIS WATERCOLOUR PAINTING of the so-called Coach Entrance (or Kennington Lane Entrance) to Vauxhall Gardens (*Fig.1*) surfaced in a private collection in the United States. The owner, who inherited the collection from her mother, offered the painting for sale on a well-known online auction site. It is now back in the UK and is the subject of ongoing research; this essay is the first result.

Vauxhall Gardens' Coach Entrance was situated at the south-west corner of the Gardens, overlooking Kennington Lane (in the foreground of the picture), roughly on the spot where the Royal Vauxhall Tavern stands today. It would have been a famous local landmark, even to people who had never visited the Gardens. It was built around 1830, replacing a simpler earlier structure (*Fig.2*), and was demolished with the rest of the gardens in 1859.

It is known from a group of 1850s watercolours that the Coach Entrance of the final decades of Vauxhall's life was a small and relatively simple building (*Fig.3*). It was little more than a frontage with a covered colonnade to shelter pedestrians and a central pediment bearing the royal coat of arms; there were kiosks behind the façade for the door-keepers, with a covered way leading into the Gardens; like many of its fellows at Vauxhall, the building was made entirely of timber. Its purpose, as the name suggests, was to provide a convenient entrance to

THE COACH ENTRANCE

FIG.1 Anonymous watercolour of 'The Coach Entrance, Royal Vauxhall Gardens'; detail of the left side of the watercolour. CVRC 0816.

the Gardens for visitors who arrived by coach. They could be dropped off at this entrance and pay their admission fee without having to walk the fifty metres or so to the main entrance through the Proprietor's House. Their vehicles would then be driven to the adjacent grassed coach park, where the horses were watered and rested before the journey home later the same evening or early the following morning. Coachmen were able to take advantage of the many local public houses, including the popular Vauxhall Tap, the Royal Oak, the George and Dragon, the Vine, Marble Hall, the Pilgrim, the Black Prince, and several other smaller inns.

Four main doorways punctuated the façade of the Coach Entrance, and the covered portico was supported on eight columns. The parapet had a number of crowned lanterns fixed to it; the boundary fence enclosing this corner of the gardens curved away to the left of the Coach Entrance, running as far as the Proprietor's House. Behind the fence were many mature trees, through which Vauxhall's Orchestra building could be discerned, but only in winter when the trees were bare.

The new watercolour agrees with this topography in general, but not in its details. It shows the building as it never quite was. The basic geography is fine, but the boundary at the south-west corner of the Gardens (to the left of the Coach Entrance building) was never a right angle, always a curve (*see Fig.5*), as the Royal Vauxhall Tavern's façade still is (*Fig.4*). Neither does the architectural detail of the yellow Coach Entrance in this new watercolour agree with any of the previously-known images, especially in its parapet design, which is more elaborate than it should be, with green panels and tapered ends (*Fig.6*). Most of the other images also show four doorways, but with a larger central opening, usually closed, making five in all, without the flanking advertising noticeboards. They invariably include eight columns supporting the portico (*see Fig.3*), rather than the six seen here.

The white house immediately to the left of the large tree (*see Fig.1*) has to be the Proprietor's (or Spring Gardens) House, but it is too small and the wrong shape. The entrance gate in front of it is in the wrong place; the corner of the Coach Field should be canted, cutting off the corner so as to make a wider splay for coaches coming out of what is now Goding Street on to Kennington Lane towards the new Vauxhall Bridge away to the left; although it may well be historically correct, the little grey 'sentry-box' on the extreme left of the image does not appear on any plan or in any other known image, and the Vauxhall Tap should

FIG.2 Detail from a wood engraving of c.1893 showing 'The Old Village of Vauxhall in 1825' looking east along Kennington Lane. The old Coach Entrance to Vauxhall Gardens is in the centre of the image.
From Edward Walford's 'Old and New London' (1893), published by Cassell Petter & Galpin, Vol. 6, p.456.

FIG.3 Reproduction from an unidentified periodical of a watercolour of the Coach Entrance in around 1850. CVRC 0395.

only have three windows on the first floor, not five. The final anomaly is the prominent Gothic turret behind the trees immediately beyond the central pediment of the yellow building. This might be thought to be the pinnacle of Vauxhall's outdoor Orchestra-stand, but it could not be—the Orchestra is well recorded in the visual documentation at all periods and it never had a turret like this on top; in any case, from this viewpoint, even the highest point of the Orchestra would be completely obscured by the trees when they were in leaf.

For an amateur topographical watercolour, these anomalies might be explained by artist's licence, by the artist misinterpreting original sketches, or by alterations and additions to Vauxhall's stock of buildings, land and attractions. An alternative explanation could be that the artist was presenting a view of what might have been—specifically a design for a new proposed building on this site. Without additional evidence, and because of the highly defined detail of the picture, this would have been the most logical interpretation of the new watercolour.

However, closer inspection of the paper on which it is painted reveals the most important clue in this puzzle; held up to the light, it can be seen that the paper has a manufacturer's watermark—'J. WHATMAN 1882' (*Fig.7*). This watermark dates the picture to more than two decades after Vauxhall Gardens closed, so it could not be a design, and must have had a very different starting-point. There is nothing about the present physical state of the watercolour to suggest that it is anything other than a genuine work from the nineteenth century, so an intentional later forgery can be ruled out. But the artist clearly did not paint this scene from life and must have invented it to look like something from fifty years earlier, based on a little bit of historical research.

An obvious feature of this picture is the trio of vehicles seen on Kennington Lane. The side-by-side two-wheeled hackney or 'coffin cab' at the left end of the building is of a type developed in the 1820s and illustrated by George Cruikshank in Charles Dickens's *Sketches by Boz* of the 1830s; the two-horse perch phaeton in the centre is a typical high-status vehicle of the same period, and, on the right, the walk-along velocipede, although still around, would have been a little old-fashioned by 1830. The costume worn by the men and women who populate this scene all back up the other details to suggest a date for the imagined scene in the 1830s, but painted half a century later.

In view of this determined retrospection, it may just have been the

THE COACH ENTRANCE

FIG. 4. The Royal Vauxhall Tavern, showing the curved frontage, on the same spot as the curved boundary fence in Fig. 5.

FIG. 5. Detail from an 1813 plan of Vauxhall Gardens showing the Coach Entrance at 'S', with the curve of the south-west boundary fence to the left. *Originally published in Owen Manning and William Bray's 'The History and Antiquities of the County of Surrey' (1804–1814), opp. p.452.*

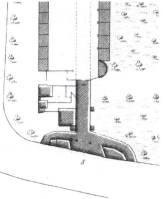

FIG.6 Detail of the right side of the watercolour shown in Fig. 1.

FIG.7 The watermark 'J. WHATMAN' with the date 1882.

work of a local painter catering to the nostalgia that certainly existed for Vauxhall Gardens at the end of the nineteenth century but, if so, it would surely have shown the inside of the Gardens, not just the utilitarian Coach Entrance. However, this very real nostalgia had several important results: it was during this late Victorian period that some of the great collections of surviving Vauxhall ephemera, now in major museums and libraries, were created. Warwick Wroth's seminal book *The London Pleasure Gardens of the Eighteenth Century*, based on his own collection (now in the Museum of London), was published in 1896, as was H.A. Rogers's *Views of Some of the Most Celebrated By-gone Pleasure Gardens of London*. The important collections of Robert Gould Shaw (Harvard Library Theatre Collection), of James Winston (Bodleian Library, Oxford), of Jacob Henry Burn and of Henry Evanion (*see p.60*) (both in the British Library), of Wroth himself, of F.W. Fairholt (Theatre Museum, London) and of other avid collectors all stem from this period, when the regret for the irrevocable loss of Vauxhall Gardens, and all that it represented, was at its most insistent.

In addition, there was one significant occasion at this time that might have prompted the creation of works like this new watercolour. This was the 'Vauxhall Revival and Bazaar' held in June 1888 at the Assembly Room of William Buxton's recently rebuilt and extended Horns Tavern at the junction of Kennington Park Road and Kennington Road (*Figs. 8, 9*).

Held under the aegis of the Women's Liberal Association, this grand event was organised by a distinguished group of patronesses headed by Catherine, the wife of the Prime Minister, William Ewart Gladstone. The Revival, which has never been fully written up, included reconstructions of Vauxhall supper-boxes where visitors could take refreshments, surrounded by illuminations and music, and imagine themselves back at Vauxhall Gardens. It also included a 'picture gallery and museum'; the museum would have displayed real 'relics' from the Gardens, such as, for instance the life-sized marble statue of Handel by Roubiliac (owned at that time by the Littleton family, of Novello's the music publishers), and some of the supper-box paintings by Francis Hayman and his studio; the 'picture gallery' would have shown images of the Gardens in their hey-day, with topographical prints of the period, but may also have included modern re-imaginings of those buildings of which no prints survived, such as the Coach Entrance itself. The present

FIG.8 Photograph of the Horns tavern as it looked after its 1887 rebuild; the assembly room is on the left of the main building.

FIG.9 The Assembly Room of the Horns Tavern, where the 1888 Vauxhall Revival was held. *Figs.8 and 9 from 'A Souvenir and History of the "Horns" Tavern Kennington', S.E., a small pamphlet published around 1935, when John Martin Booker was the proprietor.* CVRC 0827.

watercolour is carefully edge-mounted on three sides in what is now a very age-toned piece of cartridge paper–the fourth side, which may have carried information about the artist, title and date, is now sadly missing, so we have no idea who the artist was. However, the mount must have been introduced so as to make the picture presentable in a display of some sort, maybe in the Vauxhall Revival's Picture Gallery at the Horns Tavern in Summer 1888 (*Fig.9*).

As a watercolour of a later date than the building, all the 'faults' and discrepancies can be explained. All of the buildings to the west of the Gardens (the left of the picture), including the Vauxhall Tap, would have been swept away by the arrival of the railway viaduct in the 1840s; the Proprietor's House, the Coach Entrance itself, and the pleasure garden were long gone, replaced in the 1860s by three hundred terraced artisans' houses.

Memories become very fallible after thirty years, and human nature tends to idealise those views of which we hold the fondest memories. Some of the details in this watercolour, however, have the ring of truth about them–the flock of sheep grazing in the 'coach field' to keep the grass cropped, the 'sentry-box' on the left with its miniature belfry and even that problematic Gothic turret–possibly a half-remembered feature of the Gardens that had actually existed at one time, but is otherwise undocumented.

This attractive image has all the qualities we would expect of a painting done from memory by somebody who might have known the building in their younger days and has romanticised that memory because of what he or she knew was beyond it–the magical world of Vauxhall Gardens, of which they had heard so much from their parents and grandparents but probably never visited themselves. As such it is an entirely valid record of how one feature of Vauxhall Gardens was recalled by local people long after the pleasure gardens had been demolished and replaced with ten streets of houses, a church, a pub and two schools, and Vauxhall had become just another suburban district of London south of the river.

The record-breaking flight of THE ROYAL VAUXHALL BALLOON *in* 1836

A MONGST THE MANY extraordinary facts about nineteenth-century London, one stands out as almost unbelievable—an urban myth, you might think. How could the world record for manned-flight distance possibly have been set by a flight from Vauxhall—in 1836, the year before Queen Victoria came to the throne? Yet it's true. The record 480-mile flight was by the Royal Vauxhall Balloon, and took eighteen hours with three passengers and well over a ton of supplies and ballast. The record stood for almost eighty years, until February 1914, when Karl Ingold managed to cover twice the distance in a similar time in his Mercedes-powered Aviatik biplane.

The sixth flight of the Royal Vauxhall Balloon set off from Vauxhall Gardens on Monday 7 November 1836, straight into the record books. This was no publicity stunt for the popular garden resort, designated The Royal Gardens Vauxhall by Royal Warrant in 1822. November, after all, was very much in the Gardens' closed season, and there was no pre-publicity. Indeed, this flight was kept a secret until lift-off, its main purpose being experimental. Vauxhall Gardens was chosen as

---

FIG.1 'The Vauxhall Balloon'. *From 'The Mirror of Literature, Amusement and Instruction' (1836), Vol. 28, No. 796 (17 September), p.197.*

THE VAUXHALL BALLOON.

the launch-pad as it had the right facilities and because the proprietors, Frederick Gye and Richard Hughes, had commissioned and paid for the construction of the vast new balloon. It cost them around £2,100 (well over £100,000 in today's money), including about £700 (£34,000) for the silk alone, to meet the specifications of its pilot, the aeronaut Charles Green.

Green (1785–1870) was a professional balloonist. Having realised early on the disadvantages of hot air and of hydrogen as lifting agents, he had made his first ascent, in a balloon filled with coal gas, on 19 July 1821. Green eventually made over 500 balloon ascents in his career—his 500th being a perilous night flight in early September 1852, accompanied by eight passengers including the writer Henry Mayhew. By 1836, however, Green had completed 220 flights and was famed as the most experienced and expert balloonist in the country. He had designed the new 'Royal Vauxhall Balloon' not only for distance flights but also with substantial extra lifting capacity to carry passengers and equipment to conduct scientific experiments. This meant that, because of the lesser lifting-power of Green's favoured lifting-agent, coal gas, as against the more expensive hydrogen, the new balloon had to be enormous. This suited the Vauxhall Gardens proprietors, who wanted their spectacular new balloon to be as visible as possible for as long as possible after take-off. At 80 feet high and 50 feet broad (24.3 by 15.2m), this was not hard, the effect heightened by the 44 alternating crimson and white silk gores that made up the envelope of the balloon (*Fig.1*), all coated with a special varnish to prevent the escape of gas. Nearly 2,000 yards of specially-woven Spitalfields silk was used, and the other statistics, like the 85,000 cubic feet (24,000m³) of gas contained by the envelope, fall into line behind this. The original wickerwork gondola or 'car', supported by ten ropes, and draped with purple and crimson velvet, was just 9 feet by 4 feet (2.7 by 1.2m), decorated at each end with a large gilt eagle's head (*Fig.2*).

For this record-breaking flight, the gondola had to contain not only a fortnight's food and drink (in case of landing in a wilderness), but also a ton of sand ballast, much apparatus, including a 1,000-foot length of rope, a barometer and telescopes. Then there was the baggage of the three men aboard. As well as Charles Green himself, there was the Irish writer, musician and keen balloonist Thomas Monck Mason (1803–1889), who was to write a record of the journey.[35] They were

FIG. 2. Detail from a Vauxhall handbill advertising 'One More Double Ascent' on 4 September 1837, showing clearly the two eagles' heads and other features of the gondola. CVRC 0563.

accompanied by the expedition's backer, Robert Hollond (1808–1877), a lawyer and politician. Hollond was with Green on the maiden flight of the Royal Vauxhall Balloon on 9 September, when it flew twenty-six miles to beyond Gravesend in eighty minutes.

Hollond hired the balloon from the proprietors of Vauxhall Gardens for his record-breaking flight, and he paid for the necessary supplies and preparations. All three men were provided with passports for the countries in which they might land. The passport the travellers actually used, signed by Hollond, still exists and is now housed in the Cuthbert–Hodgson Collection at the National Aerospace Library at Farnborough. The balloonists' supplies of food and drink sound excessive, even for a fortnight's provision; they included forty pounds of ham, beef, and tongue, forty-five pounds of chicken, as well as preserves, sugar, bread and biscuits. On top of this, Hollond thought it necessary to stow two gallons each of sherry, port and brandy. Refreshments on this scale were likely to have been supplied by the kitchens at Vauxhall Gardens, the only London caterer of the time working on that scale.

The three men could just about squeeze into the gondola because as much stuff as possible–cloaks, bags, barometers, cordage, wine jars, spirit flasks, barrels of wood and copper, speaking trumpets, telescopes and lamps–was hung on hoops. There was also a coffee-machine, heated with slaking quick-lime. On top of everything else, the Royal Vauxhall Balloon was equipped with a 'Bengal' light (a slow-burning vivid blue firework) to lower at night to see how high they were. The base of the gondola was cushioned, in case the travellers needed to sleep, but it is hard to see that there can have been any space for them to do so, even one at a time.

FINAL PREPARATIONS FOR the great flight, the purpose of which was to test the theories formed by Green from his extensive experience, began at 7am on 7 November 1836, with the balloon being slowly filled with coal gas and the gondola with supplies. All being ready, at 1.30pm, the Royal Vauxhall Balloon took off on this sixth and most significant flight, heading south-east towards Paris. They passed over Rochester, over Canterbury, where, at 4pm they dropped a note for the mayor by parachute (the first airmail letter perhaps), and then Dover and across

FIG.3   W.J. Taylor, portrait head, in profile, of 'Charles Green Aeronaut', from the medal struck in memory of the Nassau flight, c.1837. CVRC 0506.

FIG.4   Reverse of the Nassau medal, with a balloonist's-eye-view of Weilburg, and the balloon itself, top left.

the Channel. As night fell there were some anxious moments caused by the accumulation of dew on the balloon, but Green kept the balloon aloft, and after passing Calais the trio brewed coffee on their slaked-lime stove, later amusing themselves by lowering fireworks over labourers in the fields and shouting at them through a loud-hailer to see their amazed and terrified reactions. Their journey took them over Ypres, Courtrai, Lille, Oudenaarde, Brussels, Namur, Liège (where they lost their coffee-pot), Spa, Malmedy and Koblenz.

Monck Mason's account of the flight does not say whether the men slept or not, but there was always somebody on watch. At about 3.30am, and at a height of about 12,000 feet (3,660m), the three were alarmed by three sudden explosions, which turned out to be merely the silk sections expanding in a thinner atmosphere. It was intensely cold, so they probably could not sleep in any case. They were certainly all awake before sunrise the following morning. Having passed over great tracts of snow, the party thought they might be over one of the German states or possibly even Poland, so they decided to land when they could find a suitable spot rather than risk blundering into the trackless wastes of Russia. They accordingly landed at 7.30am, and, on landing, discovered from local inhabitants who had, as Monck Mason wrote, 'for some time been shyly and timidly watching the motions of the aeronauts', that they were in the Duchy of Nassau in Germany, about six miles from the town of Weilburg, the best part of five hundred miles (805km) from London. Had they kept up speed and direction, they could easily have reached Prague the next day.

Following the descent at Weilburg, and Green's decision that the balloon had done its job, the goods from the gondola were cleared out with the help of the locals, encouraged by a 'liberal distribution of the brandy and other liquors' they had brought with them; so, by midday, they were ready to be taken to the town, where they 'experienced the kindest reception from the Prince and people of Nassau'. The church in Weilburg still boasts a stained-glass panel commemorating the event, although there is no reciprocal memorial in Vauxhall. After spending almost two weeks there, the party began their journey home–by carriage–taking note of the contrast of modes of travel, both in terms of speed and comfort. The reasonably smooth balloon flight had averaged a speed of more than 25mph (40kph), which no carriage could hope to emulate. The travellers had to make do with the coal gas already

FIG.5 'A Consultation Previous to An Aerial Voyage from London to Weilburg in Nassau.' Portraits of (left to right) Prideaux, Hollins, Milbourne James, Hollond, Monck Mason, Green. This print was originally sold for the huge price of two guineas. *(1843) Engraving by John Henry Robinson after John Hollins.*

in the balloon because they could neither transport spare gas nor make any more in inflight. Coal gas was not manufactured in Nassau, hence the return journey by land of the men and their now-deflated Royal Vauxhall Balloon.

Before returning to London, Charles Green stopped in Paris, making two ascents of the balloon there, on 19 December 1836 and on 9 January 1837 (at 1.30pm), from the Barracks on the Rue du Faubourg Poissonnière, for which Green offered seats to up to ten ladies and gentlemen as passengers. On the handbill for the first of these ascents, the balloon is called the Royal Vauxhall Nassau Balloon; on its return to Vauxhall the balloon was duly re-named the 'Nassau Balloon', and later, on 10 July 1838, under the patronage of the Duke of Nassau, the 'Royal Nassau Balloon'. The 'Duke of Nassau's Day' was celebrated at Vauxhall on that day, in the unavoidable absence of the Duke himself, who had been thrown from his horse and injured, so was unable to attend.[36]

The story of the Royal Vauxhall Balloon was retold many times over several years, and the balloon's fame spread over the whole world for its outstanding achievement. The artist J.M.W. Turner was fascinated, and pleaded with Robert Hollond to make a sketch of what he had seen—especially the tops of clouds, and how the sunlight fell. Hollond commissioned E.W. Cocks (b.1803), an in-house artist at Vauxhall Gardens, to produce a series of seven small paintings of the Weilburg flight for his private collection. Cocks himself had been a passenger on the second flight of the Royal Vauxhall Balloon, on 21 September, when it flew a mere seven or eight miles to Bromley in forty minutes.

Even though Charles Green was awarded no medal, a bronze medal was, in fact, struck in honour of his flight, with his portrait head, in profile, on the obverse, and a view of Weilburg on the reverse (*Figs. 3, 4*). This was designed and made by William Joseph Taylor (1802–1885), possibly to the commission of Robert Hollond. It is now a very scarce and precious souvenir of Green's achievement, with only five in public collections in the UK and the US together, and two or three in known private collections, which may indicate that only a few were ever produced.

At the same time as this medal was being struck, John Hollins, a artist and friend of Robert Hollond, painted a group portrait of all those involved on the venture, titled 'A Consultation Previous to An Aerial Voyage from London to Weilburg in Nassau'. Monck Mason stands at the right of a carpeted table with a map on it, with Green sitting to the right holding a telescope and Robert Hollond to the left. To the left of them stand three men – Walter Prideaux on the left grasping a walking stick in his gloved hand, with Hollins in the traditional pose of the self-portrait looking out at the viewer, and, behind Hollond, Sir William Milbourne James. Through a window, the red-and-white striped balloon can be seen ready for the ascent. Both Prideaux and James were friends of Hollond, both well-connected lawyers, and both probably involved in obtaining or drafting the necessary paperwork for the voyage. The painting, exhibited at the Royal Academy in 1838, is now in the National Portrait Gallery, London.[37] Five years later, in 1843, an expensive (presumably fund-raising) engraving was made of Hollins' painting (in the same orientation) by John Henry Robinson (*Fig.5*).

IT WAS UNFORTUNATE that the year after the Weilburg flight, on 24 July 1837, the Nassau balloon, as the only balloon capable of carrying such a weight, became the vehicle for lifting Robert Cocking's revolutionary new 'parachute' to almost a mile high before Cocking released his ludicrous machine and achieved lasting fame as the first parachute fatality in the world (*Fig.6; see also Fig.12*). After this tragic event, balloons inevitably lost some of their glamour and appeal. William Taylor had originally intended to issue his medal with two different reverse designs – the view of Weilburg on some and Robert Cocking's no less famous fatal descent on others. In the end he must have decided against this alternative reverse, as none appear to have survived.

Even though the Nassau flight may not originally have been intended as a public attraction, it inevitably became one and, in fact, the Vauxhall proprietors capitalised on this with a vast 'Grand Moving Panorama' of the voyage, to show their visitors the following year. This was not yet early cinema but a roll of painted canvas 75,500 feet long, wound between two rollers, so that about 400 feet was visible at any one time, probably about twenty or thirty feet high and probably illuminated from behind. Whether it was a view of the balloon passing over the landscape, or a continuous view from the balloon itself (as I suspect), history does not relate, but it apparently showed in fine detail the epic voyage from Vauxhall, over Chatham, Dover, the Channel, Calais, Brussels and Koblenz, and the descent near Weilburg. For those who had never been higher than a few feet or travelled more than a few miles it must have been a thrilling sight.

Following their classic flight, the three aeronauts returned to their daily lives; Robert Hollond of Stanmore Hall in Middlesex became Whig MP for Hastings, the polymath Thomas Monck Mason wrote the 52-page account of the flight. Charles Green, naturally enough, continued in his chosen profession and successfully completed 526 flights since his first on the day of the coronation of George IV in 1821, before he finally retired, after several comebacks as 'the Veteran Green', in 1854. His wife Martha (*née* Morrell) and his son George joined him in his business, as did several other members of his extended family, including his brother Harry, and themselves became successful balloonists. The family were well known to the dentist and dilettante Theodosius Purland, who wrote of them:

All his family were exceedingly illiterate and vulgar; and yet for all his vulgarity, the instant he [Charles] touched the Balloon in Vauxhall Gardens, or anywhere else, he became the gentleman and the man of science. The transformation was complete![38]

Henry Mayhew, in his vivid story about Green's eventful 500th flight, also recorded his impressions of Charles Green, 'the old ethereal pilot', after they had landed and the Nassau Balloon was all packed up. During the flight Green had been 'taciturn and almost irritable', but 'now he was garrulous, and delighting all with his intelligence, his enterprise, his enthusiasm, and his courtesy.'

On 10 September 1838 Charles Green was to achieve the records for distance (480 miles), altitude (over 27,000 feet or five miles) and possibly speed too (80mph, on the same occasion). A nice portrait of him in older age accompanied his obituary in *The Illustrated London*

FIG.6   Robert Cocking, Sketched from life in Vauxhall Gardens while superintending the preparations for his hazardous ascent July 24th. 1837.' *By 'J.H.', published by T. Pewtress, 67 Newington Causeway.*

News of 16 April 1870 (*Fig.7*). He died on 26 March that year, not aloft but at his home, Arial Villa in Holloway. He was eighty-five. The British Balloon and Airship Club named a trophy named after him, the Charles Green Salver, which is decorated with an engraving of the Nassau Balloon, and was presented to the balloonist in 1839 by Richard Crawshay, a grateful passenger. It has since been presented by the British Balloon and Airship Club for exceptional flying achievements. In recent times winners have included Richard Branson and Per Lindstrand in 1988, for the first crossing of the Atlantic by hot-air balloon, as well as to Brian Jones and Bertrand Piccard for the first round-the-world flight by balloon (1990), and no less than six times to David Hempleman-Adams between 2001 and 2012.

Of the eventual fate of the Royal Nassau Balloon itself, I can find no record. Charles Green and his family continued to fly the balloon well into the 1850s, not without both dangerous incidents (*Fig.8*)[39] and determined competition from other balloonists; the balloon made numerous appearances in song and comic poetry, and was even embroidered onto dress silk.[40] Green regularly lectured, and on 17 July 1840 bought the balloon itself from the Vauxhall proprietors for £500 at auction. He flew several other balloons at Vauxhall, all with patriotic names like the Royal Victoria, the Albion (destroyed in a crash on 20 August 1845, at Gravesend) and the Coronation (presumably created for Queen Victoria's coronation in June 1838, and always called 'Mr. Green's own balloon'). Sometimes the Green family would ascend in two balloons at the same time, just to emphasise the huge scale of the Nassau Balloon.

The Vauxhall proprietors' massive original investment in the Nassau Balloon was handsomely repaid, even in its first season, when Charles Green's balloon ascents proved a huge attraction for visitors to the Gardens. They proved be a real money-spinner in the sale of tickets for passengers to travel in the balloon's gondola on a real flight out of London. Even before the Nassau flight, on 21 September 1836, at 3.45 in the afternoon, Charles Green made the second ascent in his new balloon, with ten passengers. The proprietors had provided a new and larger gondola to accommodate more people. The charges for passengers were phenomenally high, at £21 for gentlemen (around £1,000 in today's money) and £10 10s. for ladies. Passenger tickets were also offered as prizes in Vauxhall's lotteries, with tickets selling at one shilling each.

FIG.7 Charles Green in old age. This illustration accompanied Green's obituary. *Engraved from a photograph by Mayall, published in 'The Illustrated London News' (1870), Vol. 56, No. 1589 (16 April), p.401.*

The third flight of the balloon, on 27 September, achieved the thirty-three miles to Chelmsford in less than an hour, with the ill-fated Robert Cocking as a passenger.

Vauxhall's proprietors paid Green £980 for his participation in their 1837 season, plus the income from two seats in the balloon. Even though it was not the original intention, the success of the Nassau flight gave a huge boost to the fortunes of Vauxhall Gardens in following seasons as well; it would be fair to say that Charles Green, with his regular flights, illuminated night-flights, parallel running races (following his balloon flights but on the ground), and especially his high ticket prices for passengers, was responsible for keeping the Gardens in credit when many other pleasure gardens were failing. Over the fourteen balloon days in 1838, for instance, the total income was £6,446, whereas it was only £5,544 for all the other fifty-nine nights. Illustrations of the Nassau Balloon making its ascent over the Gardens can be found in numerous journals and periodicals of the 1840s (*Fig.9*).

Monday 3 July 1854 saw the last recorded ascent of Green's Great Nassau Balloon at Vauxhall, following a lottery for six seats in the car. A year earlier, in June 1853, a brief paragraph had appeared in George Cruikshank's *Comic Almanack* satirically predicting that 'The veteran Green, by the announcement of his 8000th ascent, suspended by warranted unsafe cords, will prove that, in spite of his vast age and experience, he is not yet old enough to know better'. Even in his seventieth year, Green clearly did not consider himself so. After 1854, however, balloons drop off Vauxhall's advertising literature, although the Nassau continued to be flown elsewhere around the country; *Fig.10* shows a detail of the gondola, with twelve passengers on board, immediately before an ascent at Cremorne Gardens, Chelsea, in 1842. Another celebrated famous ballooning venue was the Montpellier Gardens in Cheltenham, where the Nassau Balloon made an ascent on 3 July 1837; ten weeks later, an unfortunate chimpanzee named Mademoiselle Jennie was dropped from the Nassau in her own 'parachute'; she survived the descent, to be reunited with her owner, the landlord of a

---

FIG.8 'Accident to the Nassau Balloon in the London Road.' The building damaged in the accident was a 'Ladies School'. *From 'The Illustrated London News' (1849), Vol. 15, No. 382 (28 July), p.61.*

THE FLIGHT OF THE ROYAL VAUXHALL BALLOON

ACCIDENT TO THE NASSAU BALLOON IN THE LONDON-ROAD, ON WEDNESDAY.

FIG.9 'Ascent of the Nassau Balloon, from Vauxhall Gardens, on Saturday' (22 June 1850) showing the balloon rising up over the stupendous three-dimensional diorama of The Kremlin, constructed on Vauxhall's 'Waterloo Ground'. *From 'The Illustrated London News' (1850), Vol. 16, No. 433 (29 June), p.464.*

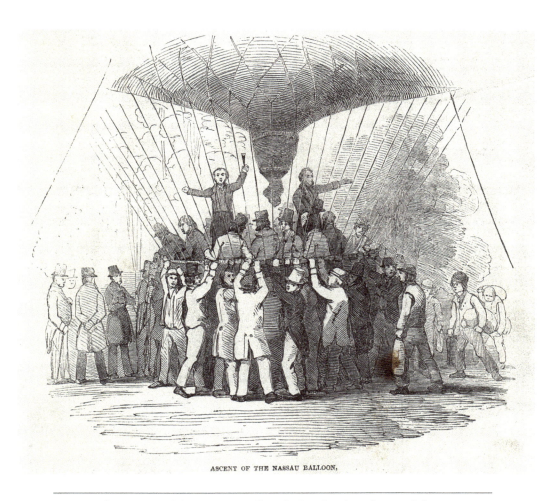

ASCENT OF THE NASSAU BALLOON.

FIG.10 'The Ascent of the Nassau Balloon', showing just the gondola, passengers and observers just before an ascent at Cremorne Gardens, Chelsea. *From 'The Illustrated London News' (1846), Vol. 9, No. 221 (25 July), p.61.*

local pub, who was probably more interested in his publicity than in her well-being. The Nassau Balloon was eventually sold to Henry Coxwell, one of Green's younger competitors, who continued using it until 1873, with some reconditioning. The likelihood is that it just became worn out after almost forty years of use and was scrapped.

Even though the phenomenal flight to Weilburg was no myth, it certainly became the stuff of myth, with stories of Charles Green having flown to the Moon, and an article in *Punch* magazine speculating on the giant balloon that could land 'a thousand troops in China in 24 hours'.[41] In the 1840s, Charles Green made plans for a transatlantic flight, never realised, which induced an Austrian printmaker, Johannes Zinke, to produce a satirical print showing Green's great balloon landed in the Antipodean Islands of the south Pacific, much to the wonder of the locals. The transatlantic flight proposal was picked up by the American writer Edgar Allan Poe, who wrote a hoax story for the *New York Sun* of 13 April 1844, trumpeting the astounding news that the Atlantic had been crossed by the balloon in just three days.[42] This brilliant hoax caused a public sensation at the time, spreading the fame of the three aeronauts throughout the United States. Charles Dickens, in his first published book, *Sketches by Boz* (1836–7), includes a description of a daytime visit to Vauxhall Gardens, during which the Green family ascend in two balloons. George Cruikshank's frontispiece illustrates the ascent of the Nassau Balloon from the Gardens, with only Charles Green and an unnamed peer aboard, cheered off by a huge and enthusiastic crowd below (*Fig.11*).

The fame of Green's Nassau balloon continues into modern times, with appearances on cigarette and trade cards in the twentieth century (*Fig.12*), on a US Air Mail first day cover in 1962, as well as postage stamp designs in Europe and America, and even, remarkably, in Mongolia in 1982 as one of a set of seven balloon-themed stamps.

Green's record-breaking flight from Vauxhall was a phenomenal achievement at a time when ballooning had become little more than a gentleman's entertainment. He pioneered the use of coal gas instead of hydrogen, he proved the efficacy of the 'trail-rope', still in use today, and he demonstrated that gas balloons were capable not only

---

FIG.11 George Cruikshank, frontispiece to Charles Dickens's *Sketches by Boz*, Series 2, of 1837.

THE FLIGHT OF THE ROYAL VAUXHALL BALLOON

ESSAYS ON VAUXHALL GARDENS

FIG.12 A trade card produced by Patersons of Edinburgh, plumbers, c.1960, showing the ascent of the Nassau Balloon with Robert Cocking's parachute suspended beneath it in 1837.

of safe, sustained heavier-than-air manned flight, but also of considerable speed, if the correct height could be reached, and of changing direction by changing height, so catching different winds. He also showed convincingly that passengers in a balloon did not suffer from lack of oxygen, nor were they frozen solid by the colder air, both fears that had been expressed by other aeronauts. Under Green's expert leadership, ballooning became safer and more controllable than before. More than anything, however, it is thanks to Charles Green that ballooning became the serious and respectable occupation and sport it still is today.[43]

Tracking THE FATE *of the* VAUXHALL GARDENS BANDSTAND

A T THEIR DISPOSAL sale of the 'Fixtures, Fittings, and Building Materials of the Royal Gardens, Vauxhall', on 22 August 1859, the auctioneers, Messrs. Samuel and Robert C. Driver of Whitehall, sold as lot 125 (*Fig.1*):

> The entire erection of the elegant Circular Orchestra with minarets, leaded cupola roof, and gallery, American, Stout and Oyster Bars, with the fittings, shelves, and 2 beer engines and pipes, metal top counter, stairs frontispiece, and pipes, and machinery of organ, bellows, & 2 figures on pedestals, supporting shell sounding-board, 4 looking-glass panels, &c., &c.

At the auction, which took place at the Gardens, the Orchestra building fetched £99, but no record was kept of the purchaser. Its current whereabouts are unknown. The Orchestra or bandstand had stood on that spot, in the centre of the Grove at Vauxhall Gardens, which was by 1859 'Royal Gardens, Vauxhall', for more than a century, since 1754 (*see Fig.3*). During that time it had undergone several major alterations and many refurbishments, but basically it was the same structure that Jonathan Tyers himself had commissioned to replace his original rather uninteresting outdoor Orchestra-stand. The new

ROYAL GARDENS, VAUXHALL.

FIRST PORTION OF THE SALE OF THE FIXTURES, FITTINGS, PLANT, AND MATERIALS.

A CATALOGUE

OF THE VALUABLE

Fixtures, Fittings, and Building Materials,

OF THE

ROYAL GARDENS, VAUXHALL,

CONSISTING OF

**THEATRE, ORCHESTRA, DANCING PLATFORM,
FIREWORK GALLERY,
FIGURES OF NEPTUNE AND SEA HORSES,**

FOUNTAINS, STATUES, VASES, GROTTO WORK,

FITTINGS OF ROTUNDA,

COFFEE ROOM, AND SUPPER BOXES,

ENGINE HOUSE, WITH ENGINE, GEAR, SAWS, &C.

GASOMETER AND RETORTS,

ABOUT SIXTY-ONE IRON COLUMNS,

Large Square and Circular Tables, Forms, Seats with Backs, Cane Seated Chairs, Gas Fittings, and a Variety of Miscellaneous Articles and Effects.

The whole to be disposed of, in consequence of its being decided to Let this Valuable Freehold Property for

BUILDING PURPOSES.

WHICH WILL BE SOLD BY AUCTION,

BY MESSRS. DRIVER,

ON THE PREMISES,

On **MONDAY**, **AUGUST** 22nd, at Eleven for Twelve o'clock precisely.

May be Viewed, Three days previous to the Day of Sale, by Admission Catalogues, Sixpence each (to be returned to Purchasers), to be had of the Manager, at the Office of the Vauxhall Gardens Estate ; at the Auction Mart, London ; and of Messrs. DRIVER, Surveyors, Land Agents, and Auctioneers, 5, Whitehall, London, S.W.

FIG.1   The Drivers' sale catalogue for the auction of 22 August 1859. CVRC 0506.

building would have been known by all the great Vauxhall musicians from Handel onwards (*Fig.2*).

The various bars that Mr. Driver tells us are housed in the ground floor of the Gothic building were recent makeshift additions to the noble old building, as was the ice cream bar which is visible in an extraordinary photograph taken in 1859 and preserved in the Lambeth Archives.[44] More worthy additions were the great 'shell' sounding-board, added in 1824 by the Gardens' carpenter Thomas Lowe, and supported on two huge decorative lyres set on top of sculpted drums.

That year the Orchestra was repainted in pink, white and gold. In 1845 the lyres and drums were replaced with draped female figures or caryatids on pedestals to support the shell, during the overhaul and redecoration of the building carried out by the chief painter and decorator, Mr Hurwitz, 'in the most costly taste' (*Fig.4*). If nothing else survives of the Orchestra, these two supporting figures may do so; it was suggested that they might have been re-used in the portico of the Tate South Lambeth Library in South Lambeth Road (long ago removed), which had its own pairs of caryatids supporting the small roof, but those figures, according to contemporary prints, were rather different.

The great shell sounding board can be seen lying on the ground in a watercolour by James Findlay in the Museum of London, painted on the spot while the building was being demolished for removal in November 1859. It is obvious from this and other late views of the Orchestra that the building was in less than pristine condition, extensively oil-stained and scorched from the illuminations, and that it would have needed considerable restoration to be re-erected somewhere else. But presumably, the fact that somebody paid almost £100 for it suggests that it was destined for a new use, rather than merely scrap or firewood. The organ would have been worth something, even after a century of hard use, the lead from the cupola would have had some value too, and even the bar-room equipment may have been worth preserving, but £99 would have bought all of that as new, and more besides, so it is probable that the building was intended for a life of its own after Vauxhall closed.

Maybe it was re-used at another pleasure garden, either in this country or overseas. There were so-called 'Vauxhalls' all over the world, mostly short-lived and mostly fairly disreputable, but there may have been one or two with higher aspirations, even one that was started up by a member of Vauxhall's own staff, finding himself out of work.

THE FATE OF THE VAUXHALL GARDENS BANDSTAND

FIG.2 Detail from A Perspective View of the Grand Walk in Vauxhall Gardens, and the Orchestra. *Published in 'The Gentleman's Magazine' (1765).*

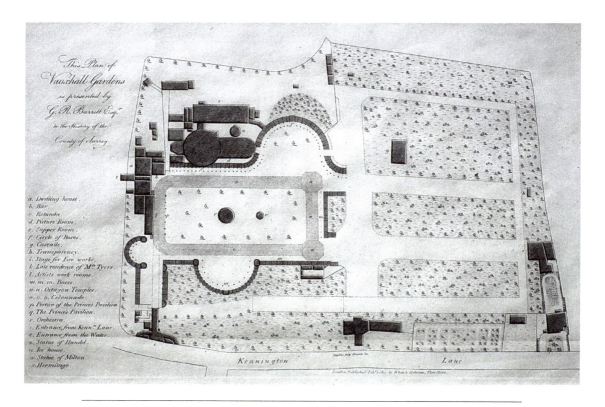

FIG.3 William Simpkins, Measured ground-plan of Vauxhall Gardens in 1813, with the Orchestra in the centre of the rectangular Grove, marked with an 'r'. CVRC 0008.

Some staff members are known to have emigrated to the USA and to Australia. Most of the UK Vauxhalls had closed by 1859, so it may be more fruitful to look further afield; the USA had many Vauxhalls, in Charleston, Nashville, Baltimore and Philadelphia, but especially in New York where a pleasure garden called the Palace Gardens was developed from 1858, very much inspired by the earlier pleasure gardens; Palace Gardens were built on an open lot between Fourteenth and Fifteenth Streets, New York, by Cornelius V. Deforest and his partner called Tisdale. Here they even erected 'a large, two-level octagonal orchestra, a fireworks platform and several arbours'. This orchestra is shown in an 1858 print,[45] and it is probably not the Vauxhall Orchestra, although not so different either, suggesting that, even though the Vauxhall Gardens Orchestra was over a century old, its shape and size would still have been acceptable to a later nineteenth-century audience.

In Australia and New Zealand, Vauxhalls, Cremornes and Ranelaghs came and went with surprising rapidity through the nineteenth century–Adelaide, Kalgoorlie, Perth, and, of course, Sydney and Melbourne all have well-recorded pleasure gardens. The best known of the Antipodean gardens was the 'Vauxhall' at Dunedin in the South Island of New Zealand, founded by Henry Farley in 1862. A Mr C. Farley had directed the re-enactments of the Battle of Waterloo at London's Vauxhall in the 1820s and 1830s–maybe Henry was a relative.

One of the best set-up pleasure gardens in Australia was Cremorne Gardens (named for the successful gardens in Chelsea) in the Melbourne suburb of Richmond, founded in 1856; here £60,000 was invested by George S. Coppin in his new venture. Coppin was consciously trying to emulate London's Vauxhall, and his nostalgic entertainments included 'Golden Age' fireworks, with balloon ascents, music and dancing; he even emulated Vauxhall's great illuminated dioramas, showing the 'Siege of Sebastopol' with artillery and fireworks in 1856. Might he have wanted to re-erect the old Orchestra at his new pleasure garden? He certainly had the capital to do so.

Melbourne is absolutely the kind of city where Vauxhall's old Orchestra could so easily have reappeared; it is probable that other features of Vauxhall Gardens had already found their way there in the 1860s; the numerous statues displayed from before 1864 to the 1930s in Melbourne's Fitzroy Gardens, some of which look very like statues known to have been installed at Vauxhall in the 1820s, were sold at the same sale (lots 129–134) as the Vauxhall Orchestra. Did the buyer take them out to Melbourne, and did the same buyer also acquire the Orchestra, dismantle it and pack it up, and then transport it 10,500 miles to a new home and a new life? Having paid the equivalent of five hundred days' skilled wages for the old building, maybe he did. It would surely have been a worthwhile investment as a good selling-point for his new business. There was widespread 'homesickness' among emigrants who found themselves cut off from English culture and English history, so any link with 'home' would have been treasured and much visited. Many emigrants would have known Vauxhall before leaving England, and reports of events at Vauxhall were carried in the Australian and New Zealand press until its closure, so everybody would have heard of it even if they did not know of it personally. Australia still has an outstanding array of fine park bandstands, largely built between the 1870s and 1920s and beautifully maintained today, which are the direct descendants of Vauxhall's Orchestra, helping new immigrants to feel at home (*Fig.5*).

Both the Vauxhall and Fitzroy Gardens statues were cast from artificial stone, painted white; such objects would not have been easily available in Melbourne at the time, so were worth the considerable cost and difficulty of transporting them from London. Most of the statues were unremarkable classical standing figures, usually female, emblematic of the seasons or of mythological characters. The one distinctive piece portrays 'Diana arresting the Flying Hart'. This same subject had been installed, the same size and precisely the same model, at Vauxhall, and appears in an engraving of the Ballet Theatre in the 1840s (*Fig.6*).

Whether the two were identical or not is still open to conjecture, but there appears to be no compelling evidence against the possibility. The eventual disposal of the Fitzroy statues may have been brought about by the difficulty and expense of maintenance, once the artificial stone began to break down, more than a century after their manufacture (*Fig.7*).

FIG.4 George Cruikshank's 'Vauxhall Gardens by Day', published in Charles Dickens's *Sketches by Boz* (1836), shows the sculpted lyres and drums below the shell. The singers of the 'plaintive duet' are probably 'Billy' Williams and Miss Forde.

THE FATE OF THE VAUXHALL GARDENS BANDSTAND

VAUXHALL GARDENS BY DAY.

FIG.5 'The 'Rotunda' bandstand in King Edward Park, Newcastle, New South Wales, built to the designs of Englishman Alfred Sharp in 1898.

THE FATE OF THE VAUXHALL GARDENS BANDSTAND

FIG.6   The Ballet Theatre and Entrance to the Grand Walk at Vauxhall in 1841. This is an unusual published image of the Diana statue in its original site. *From Charles Knight's 'London' (1841), Vol. 1. p.412.*

FIG.7   Central Avenue, Fitzroy Gardens, Melbourne; a postcard of c.1910, showing the Diana statue and one other.

FIG.8 The Vauxhall Orchestra at the close of the gardens in 1859. The two caryatids are clearly visible supporting the shell sounding-board in this topographically accurate view. *From Edward Walford's 'Old and New London' (1878), Vol. 4, p.451.*

If the Orchestra did not find its way to Melbourne with the statues, there are at least two other possible Antipodean stopping-points, whether at Kohler's Vauxhall in Canterbury, New Zealand, launched in 1860, or William Colby's Vauxhall Gardens in Auckland a few years later. Both are poorly recorded in the visual documentation, so it is not obvious what sort of architecture they included.

Taverns, parks and suburbs named Vauxhall are found world-wide; these are sometimes all that remains of a public garden or concert-room; Marseille and Arles in the south of France both have Vauxhalls; places as diverse as Barbados, Brussels, Toronto, Stockholm and Pavlovsk too. These would appear to be unlikely candidates for acquiring the Vauxhall Orchestra, particularly when the start-dates for the Australian and New Zealand gardens coincide so closely with the end-date of Vauxhall itself, and others do not. On the other hand, there is no accounting for the eccentricity of that one Vauxhall *aficionado* who became so obsessed with the Gardens that he wanted to keep the iconic Orchestra building himself for no obvious reason other than sentimental attachment. One such might be John Fillinham, one of the great collectors of Vauxhall memorabilia, who with his friends Theodosius Purland and F.W. Fairholt attended the 'last night forever' and heard the tenor Russell Grover sing 'Nevermore' to close the evening.

The Orchestra may still be languishing, in pieces, in a warehouse just metres from its original site, or it may have been taken to the other side of the world, or else it may not have survived at all. If this is the case, though, was any relic preserved? The old organ's keyboard, the caryatids, the shell-shaped sounding board, a gothic pinnacle from the roof, or just a music-stand, all visible in the illustration, are all possible survivals.[46]

MEASUREMENTS AND MONEY
1 foot = 0.3m; 1 yard = 0.9m; 1 mile = 1.6km; 1 gallon = 4.5l

A guinea is 21 shillings (a pound and a shilling).

£100 to a skilled tradesman or a household servant would have been two years' wages, or would have bought six horses, eighteen cows, or 151 stones of wool.

PICTURE CREDITS
All images, unless stated otherwise, are taken from originals in David E. Coke's own Vauxhall Gardens collection and are copyright to that collection.

The images from Cruikshank's *Comic Almanack* (1842) on pages 16 and 26 © J.J. Visser and are reproduced with his kind permission.

The London Sights game on page 41 © Foundling Museum.

ACKNOWLEDGEMENTS
David Coke acknowledges the kind assistance and hard work of Dr Alan Borg, Karen Coke, and Dr Pieter van der Merwe MBE, DL of the Royal Museums, Greenwich.

NOTES

1   *Sculpture Journal* (2007), Vol. 6, Part 2, pp.5–22.

2   *London Journal* (2016), Vol. 41, No. 1, pp.17–35.

3   *Gentleman's Magazine* (1836), Vol. 5, Feb, p.210.

4   William Clarke (1827), *Every Night Book, or, Life After Dark*. London: T. Richardson, p.187.

5   Lambeth Archives, Vauxhall Gardens Albums 5, f.226.

6   Lambeth Archives, Vauxhall Gardens Albums 5, f.185.

7   Harvard Theatre Collection, Shaw Collection, Vol.3, p.35.

8   Unidentified cutting in the J.H. Burn collection, British Library, Cup.401.K7, f.445.

9   Harvard Theatre Collection, Shaw Collection, Vol. 3, p.90.

10   *The Magazine of Curiosity and Wonder*, 7 Jan 1836, p.82.

11   Jonathan or Jonas Blewitt (1782–1853) was principal composer to Vauxhall between 1828 and 1839.

12   Harvard Theatre Collection, Shaw Collection, Vol. 9, pp.198–200.

13   Image is available online at the Look and Learn History Picture Library (ref. XJ 132589).

14   Lambeth Archives, Vauxhall Gardens Albums 4, f.211.

15   Jerry Abershaw was a highwayman hanged in chains at Kennington Common in 1795.

16   Unidentified cutting of 17 Aug 1835, Lambeth Archives, Vauxhall Gardens Albums 2, f.10.

17   Lambeth Archives, Minet Vauxhall Gardens, Vol. 2, f.82.

18   MG 691.

19   David E. Coke and Alan Borg (2011). *Vauxhall Gardens, A History*. Yale University Press, p.353.

20   Visit Adrian Seville's website giochidelloca.it for his database of 2,500 examples of antique board games.

21   It is poorly reproduced in the 'John Bologna' entry in P.H. Highfill, K.A. Burnim and E.A Langhan's *A Biographical Dictionary of Actors, Actresses, Musicians, Dancers, Managers & other Stage Personnel in London 1660–1800*. Carbondale & Edwardsville: Southern Illinois University Press (1973), Vol. 2, p.190.

22   *Universal Magazine of Knowledge and Pleasure* (1807), Vol. 7, No. 38 (January), p.62, which includes a rather sniffy criticism of the production, as beneath the critic's serious notice, despite the audience's rapturous response.

23   Galleries at 207–9, Regent Street exhibiting views of famous places across the world.

24   Intaglio is a printing process based on an etched or incised plate; letterpress prints from raised type and blocks.

25   Henry Hutchinson Montgomery (1889), *The History of Kennington and its Neighbourhood*. London: Stacey Gold, p.86.

26   Harvard Theatre Collection, TS 952.2F.

27   James Black Findlay, 'Evanion', *The Sphinx* (1950), Vol. 48, No.11 (Jan), pp.291–4.

28   Elizabeth Harland, 'The Evanion Collection', *British Library Journal* (1987), Vol. 13, No. 1 (Spring), p.65, available at www.bl.uk/eblj/1987articles/pdf/article5. pdf; Post Office Directories, 1875–1890.

29 Findlay, *op.cit.*, p.291.

30 Findlay, *op.cit.*, illustrations, pp.293, 294.

31 Lambeth Archives, George Stevens's Vauxhall account books, W/162/7.

32 See Stanford's six-inch Library Map of London and its Suburbs (1862).

33 A dressmaker specialising in ladies' tailoring.

34 Harry Houdini [Erik Weisz] (1908), *The Unmasking of Robert-Houdin*. New York: The Publishers Printing Co.

35 Thomas Monck Mason's *An Account of the Late Aeronautical Expedition from London to Weilburg, Accomplished by Robert Hollond Esq., Monck Mason, Esq., and Charles Green, Aeronaut,* published in London by F.C. Westley, in 1836, and by Theodore Foster in New York, in 1837. An enlarged illustrated version called *Aeronautica*, with five lithographic plates and a frontispiece, was published in London by F.C. Westley in 1838.

36 Vauxhall Gardens Wine Account Book, 53.32/1.

37 John Hollins, A Consultation prior to the Aerial Voyage to Weilburg, 1836, NPG 4710.

38 Cyril Bowdler-Henry (1962). *The Unique Scrap-books of Theodosius Purland*, MA, PhD, 1805-1881. London: Royal College of Surgeons, p.11.

39 One such accident was reported in *The Illustrated London News* (1849), Vol. 15, No. 382 (28 July), p.13; reported in the *Daily National Intelligencer* of Washington (USA), on 15 August.

40 A gentleman's silk waistcoat, embroidered with a repeating balloon motif, clearly the Nassau Balloon, was sold at Tennants Auctions, North Yorkshire on 29 April 2016.

41 *Punch* (1842), Vol. 3, No. 65, p.155.

42 *The Sun* (New York) (1844), p.1.

43 For further information, see Tim Robinson's 2012 article 'Balloon Pioneer Charles Green' at aerosociety.com/news/balloon-pioneer-charles-green-the-parachuting-monkey

44 Lambeth Archives, Minet Vauxhall Gardens, Vol. 6, f.167.

45 The Miriam and Ira D. Wallach Division of Art, Prints and Photographs: Print Collection, The New York Public Library. 'The Palace Garden (with accompaniment of singing bird.)' (1858).

46 If you know of any structure that could be the Vauxhall bandstand, please contact David E. Coke through his website vauxhallgardens.com.

Lightning Source UK Ltd.
Milton Keynes UK
UKHW050312020622
403841UK00003B/59